ESTHER DEANS

NO-DIG GARDENING
LEAVES OF LIFE

HarperCollins*Publishers*

HarperCollins*Publishers*

First published in Australia in 1994
This edition first published in 2001
by HarperCollins*Publishers* Pty Limited
ABN 36 009 913 517
A member of the HarperCollins*Publishers* (Australia) Pty Limited Group
http://www.harpercollins.com.au

HarperCollins*Publishers*
25 Ryde Road, Pymble, Sydney NSW 2073, Australia
31 View Road, Glenfield, Auckland 10, New Zealand
77–85 Fulham Palace Road, London W6 8JB, United Kingdom
Hazelton Lanes, 55 Avenue Road, Suite 2900, Toronto, Ontario M5R 3L2
and 1995 Markham Road, Scarborough, Ontario M1B 5M8 Canada
10 East 53rd Street, New York NY 10022, USA

National Library of Australia Cataloguing-in-Publication data:

Deans, Esther.
  No-dig gardening ; Leaves of life.
  ISBN 0 7322 7099 5.
  1. Gardening. 2. No-tillage. 3. Gardening for the handicapped.
  4. Vegetable gardening. 5. Organic gardening.
  6. Gardening – Therapeutic use. I. Deans, Esther. Esther
  Deans' gardening book. II. Deans, Esther. Leaves of life.
  III. Title. IV. Title : Leaves of life.
635

Cover photo by Ed Ramsay for *Good Gardening* magazine
Cover and internal design by Judi Rowe, HarperCollins Design Studio
Typeset by HarperCollins Design Studio in 11/14 Sabon
Printed in Australia by McPherson's Printing Group on 79gsm Bulky Paperback White

5 4 3 2 1   01 02 03 04

CONTENTS

ESTHER DEANS' STORY

When I was a child, I remember how much I enjoyed being rewarded for a job well done. I remember receiving a pat on the back with a hearty 'good girl', or that little gift left to be discovered on the bed — surprise, surprise — for doing well in exams, or the promise of a special treat for giving a helping hand when needed.

Yes, I remember, and looking back now and in the years to come I will say 'thanks for the memories', for the many wonderful experiences, for the thousands of people young and old, from all walks of life, who have shared this time with me. I will also be thankful for the opportunity to visit many places, for the hundreds of folk I have not yet met but with whom I have corresponded and for the tremendous interest and support from the media. Above all thanks a thousand times to the good Lord who prepared and guided me in all I have done.

Life is exciting and there is much to do. It is beholden to every right-thinking person to see that our children learn to love our beautiful world: to understand the wonders of creation, the soil, the water, the sun and moon, the rainbow, the magic of the wind and the rolling sea; to understand the miracle of their own bodies, their needs and how to keep healthy and happy.

Back in 1977 on an open garden day, Jan and John Miller came to meet a dear friend in my garden. Their friend felt the garden would give her something fresh to think about as her son had recently died. John was a scout for Rigby's, the publishers, and two weeks later he rang up to invite me to write a book about my backyard garden. He asked me to write just as I talked to the people visiting my garden. What a surprise! I had answered many letters and written articles, but I had never written a book.

John suggested I write the first chapter and supply headings for the following chapters. The family said 'Give it a go, Mum'. A challenge is always exciting, so I decided to 'give it a go'. For two whole weeks it was sheer agony waiting for inspiration and trying to make a start. On a Tuesday night, exactly two weeks later, I decided it was to be that night or never. By 11 p.m. there was still no mark on the paper; at 1.45 a.m. I put my pen down. It was no use, I did not know how to start to write a book. With a feeling of agitation I went to the kitchen to make myself a hot drink, but before I got there the inspiration came as I thought: 'Why do we want to have a garden?' That was it! I went back to write down the heading, and my pen did not stop until 3.30 a.m. — words just flowed on and on. I was truly guided. Subsequent headings were not difficult: garden making, herbs, seeds, creatures in the garden, planting time etc.

John was delighted, but Rigby's rejected it, which turned out to be the best thing that could have happened. John took the book to Harper and Row and it became the first book they published in Australia.

By November 1977, the *Esther Deans' Gardening Book: Growing Without Digging* had been printed. When Mr Watson, manager of Harper and Row, presented me with the first book off the press he said: 'What better way to put our grass roots down than [with] a little garden book?'

I decided to give two-thirds of my royalties for the book to the spastic children who could not run on the soft warm earth, and to the blind children who could not see the wonder of all creation.

On Sunday, 13 November 1977, my book was dedicated to service and the next day it was launched at St Ives Shopping Centre. It was a very simple, friendly gathering hosted by the local bookshop and I shared the occasion with relatives, friends and shoppers. By the end of the day, 317 books had been autographed. By the end of December 1977 two more printings, each of 5000, were made. Little did I imagine that by October 1990 82,500 copies of that little book would have been printed.

It was a very exciting time following the launch, with book signing promotions, giving talks and showing many visitors my garden. I was also honoured by Sir Garfield

Barwick, who presented me with a certificate awarding me Life Membership of The Royal New South Wales Institution for Deaf and Blind Children.

After the success of the gardening book, I was asked in 1978 to write another book, *Esther Deans' Garden Cook Book — From Garden to Kitchen*. I enjoy preparing vegetables for our family meals and making up new recipes, so this book was not as much of a problem to begin as the gardening book had been. Once again, Harper and Row were the publishers and it was publicly launched at St Ives Shopping Centre. The royalties from the 12,500 copies printed were shared with the Multiple Sclerosis Society and the Lorna Hodgkinson Sunshine Home, plus others who needed help.

It was requested that both books be transcribed into braille by Miss Betty Burr of Brisbane. I had no idea this was happening until I was invited to a meeting at the Queensland Braille Writing Association at Annerley, Queensland, to receive copies. I was completely overwhelmed. Since that day many copies in braille have been sent to other countries, and to various schools and individuals as gifts. It was being printed by the Braille Press in Edinburgh when I was there in 1981, and a copy was sent to St Johns, Newfoundland.

There was also a request from a young man in Brisbane

who was visually impaired, to have my books recorded on cassette. Many recorded copies have been made since then — and sent as far away as Kenya — and in Sydney tapes were made for the Print Handicapped Library.

Interviews for television, radio, magazines and newspapers; invitations to speak about the *no-dig garden* throughout the country — in Sydney, Perth, Adelaide and Melbourne — and in New Zealand, all helped to spread the message to people who wanted to have gardens without digging. Many excited and wonderful stories could be told about gardens made at various schools and centres for people with handicaps; about gardens made on table tops, on old beds, on rock, hard clay and sand; of gardens made on old carpet, on old coats from a shearing shed, on concrete under a clothes hoist, as well as on black oily soil in Houston, Texas. People in all walks of life have enjoyed making gardens without digging.

Because I no longer live in St Ives and have my beautiful vegetable garden, I can look back and appreciate how the years of working in the garden helped restore my health — and give thanks for all the wonderful things that happened during those years. Now I can say 'thanks for the memories' and thanks again for the opportunity to create different gardens in the retirement village where I now live. Gardens in the Nursing Centre, where the elderly residents can enjoy the flowers and their fragrances, are referred to as 'Esther's Therapy Gardens' — this is quite exciting.

How humble and privileged all this has made me feel, and I ask why the good Lord chose me, a little backyard gardener, to be able to help so many people.

NO-DIG GARDENING

This book is dedicated to the spastic children
who cannot run on the soft warm earth,
and to the blind children who cannot see
the wonders of creation.

FOREWORD

Esther Deans' *no-dig garden* has been an inspiration to so many people, showing them how to grow plants and how to enjoy them, not by battling with Mother Nature but by cooperating with her. They have discovered peace and happiness in the garden by accepting nature as a friend rather than an opposing force.

Some practices I do not understand, perhaps because there is at this stage no accepted scientific explanation for them, but they are producing results without involving much effort or expense.

The no-dig principle I accept fully. I have for many years protested that it is so wrong to bury living soil. Healthy surface soil is certainly alive, teeming with organisms busily converting organic matter into plant foods. Some of these useful organisms also inhibit or prevent development of parasitic fungi responsible for plant disease.

In nature, spent plant material or other organic waste is deposited on the soil surface. Obviously the great population of microscopic creatures concerned with the recycling of organic material was also intended to live in or on the surface soil, not at spade depth.

Our friends the earthworms with their constant tunnelling will supply the aeration needed by plant roots in any healthy soil receiving a continuous supply of organic matter. Earthworms also extend the depth of top soil by pulling decomposed organic material to lower depths and bringing soil from lower levels to the surface.

Esther Deans explains how to start a successful hay and straw garden on the surface of the toughest soil, at the same time improving the latter. This most unconventional type of garden can even be started on solid concrete.

Hoping that you find the key to more successful and happier gardening in this book.

the late Allan Seale

ESTHER DEANS AND HOME GARDENING

Why do we want to have a garden? I believe it is the Love of growing things, of watching the wonders of Nature unfold before our eyes. To see the fascinating results of a tiny seed yielding its beauty in colour, form and fragrance. Fragrance in many forms: sweet perfume from the tiny violet, the honey smell, the delightful culinary scent of herbs. We so often pass by without thinking of these wonders. The brilliance of the red poinsettia, the soft glorious blue of the jacaranda tree, the bright yellow of the daffodil.

Rest for a while in your garden and let your thoughts wander at random to ponder on its beauty. You will be surprised at how relaxed you will feel after a short time. Think of the creatures we find in our gardens — the beauty of the butterfly; the swift flight of the birds, the joy of hearing them chatter and sing; the minute insects under stones and plants; our hardworking friend the earthworm; and even the caterpillar who enjoys eating our tender plants!

Many books have been written about home gardens, compost gardens, organic gardens, bio-dynamic gardens, hydroponic gardens, and so on. In this book I want to talk of the most important of all: a garden made with Love, with a capital 'L'. A garden of vital and healthy plants to provide food for our own health. Hippocrates stressed the importance of good taste and variety: 'If the musician composed a piece of music all on one note, it would fail to please.'

The same applies to our food. We should eat as great a variety of natural, fresh, unprocessed food, especially fruit and vegetables, so that over seven days our mineral and vitamin intake pleases our body and gives us the good health to enjoy a full and active life. The home garden is Nature's answer!

My gardening philosophy is that one should be able to enjoy the results of successful vegetable growing, as well as other plants, without tiresome 'spade' work. Gardens are not made by sitting in the shade and saying, 'Oh how beautiful!', but neither need they be made with hours of backbreaking toil. The actual construction of my kind of garden is described in this book, and is simplicity itself. But briefly, the garden is made on top of the existing ground, using newspaper, lucerne hay, straw and compost. It does not require any digging to build, or to maintain. Given the right conditions, Nature is only too pleased to do most of the work for you. This garden can be made and enjoyed by old people, the handicapped, as well as all of those whose busy daily program does not allow them the time to spend hours in the backyard.

A usual question asked of me when speaking to a group of gardeners either at home or at a meeting is, 'What made you start a garden like this?' Maybe it will help you not to be discouraged about a poor sick garden if I tell you the story.

Some years ago I was very ill, almost bedridden, and many items of food were wrong for me. My body was not getting enough of the correct nourishment. At the time we had only one vegetable garden of imported sandy loam. How like my own life it was — sick and undernourished. My love of the earth and growing things began to come back to me. I could feel the need to start gardening and decided to try to regain my health through eating as many home-grown vegetables as possible. Exercising in the sun and rain and contact with the earth has worked wonders for me.

The old garden was quite depleted of humus and the white grubs had so multiplied that they presented a real problem. The Department of Agriculture advised poison to eradicate them, but by this time I had learned about poisons and their injurious effect on our gardens, so I gently worked the soil until all the grubs had gone. It came repeatedly to my mind that I should use lucerne hay, remembering what I had read years before about the wonderful qualities of this plant. As lucerne grows, its deep roots bring up from the earth minerals, trace elements and other valuable nutriments which make the hay useful to the plants in our garden. I ordered some from the local produce store. When the man came to deliver the first bale of lucerne hay to me, he looked around the garden for the horse! When I told him that it was for the garden, he stared at me with a very questioning gaze. Many bales have been delivered uneventfully since that day.

I covered the area of the garden to be restored with the pads of lucerne hay as they came from the bale, gathered some earthworms to put beneath the pads, spread a little compost over the top and started watering. It wasn't long before the earthworms began to work in the hay and multiply. For six weeks we watched this area and then planted bean seeds. The results were splendid. Encouraged, I started on the next section, restoring the remainder of the garden in the same manner.

This was the genesis of my *no-dig garden*! A garden is something to be enjoyed and shared. Over the years much knowledge has been gained by experiments. We are learning and improving all the time, hence the garden described to you in this book is different (and easier) than the original prototype of many years ago. I have graduated from 'L-Plates' but am still on 'P-Plates', always discovering new and wonderful things.

In fact, the experiences that have flowed into my life as a direct result of success with my garden have literally changed the way I live. So many wonderful and enriching things have occurred. The initial success of the first garden I built according to the plan in this book, that is, the first one after the prototype I have just described, was most encouraging. The best yield from it was 22½ kilograms (49½ pounds) of potatoes from an area measuring two and a half metres long by one and three quarter metres wide — two and a half square metres (eight feet by six feet — 48 square feet), and this was from one planting!

Members of a local gardening club heard from a friend about my garden and expressed a wish to come and see it. I was delighted that they were interested and after their visit word of mouth spread and more requests were received not only from gardening clubs, but Senior Citizens' Clubs, Ladies Auxiliaries and the like. It seemed that people were interested. I started a Visitors' Book to keep a record of my visitors. As more people found out about my methods, I found myself writing small articles for magazines in response to requests from editors. The project gained momentum. My garden was visited by reporters, and written about in newspapers and more magazines. I was asked to speak on gardening programs on the radio and a number of television segments have been made on the garden in both Australia and New Zealand. Perhaps the biggest thrill was when I was visited by Keith Smith, a radio journalist who broadcast Radio Australia short wave on the BBC. We spent a long time talking, he made a tape, signed the Visitors' Book and left. Imagine when a friend rang me at six a.m. one morning to say that he had just heard an international broadcast in which there was a segment about my *garden without digging*. I was happy to share something which had brought me such happiness and health.

I first opened the garden in 1975; there have been visitors to it ever since. In 1975 I was awarded the Championship Ribbon for vegetables at the Ku-ring-gai Horticultural Society Show, as well as first and second prizes for two dahlias I had entered. There is an amusing story about the dahlias. As I was picking the vegetables on the morning of the show I noticed two exquisite dahlias growing among the vegetables. I like to have flowers in the vegetable garden for colour, and of course it brings the bees who are pollinators. On a whim, I picked the two dahlias and decided to enter them.

Arriving at the show there were many flower exhibitors

ushering in their best examples, all protected in boxes against the wind and looking very practised and professional. There was I simply marching in with two flowers in a plain vase. I entered the flowers first and then went off to attend to the business of entering all of the vegetables, which were in a different section. After the judging, I was so excited at the success of the vegetables that I forgot about the dahlias. I was overwhelmed that the two flowers I had plonked in vases on the spur of the moment had done so well.

Since that day in 1975, when I opened the garden as a result of success at the show, thousands of people have signed the Visitors' Book. This garden has now been built by hundreds of people around Australia and overseas.

The greatest success story comes from a lady who also lives in Sydney. She visited my garden one weekend and was excited by the prospect of being able to raise such wonderful vegetables without tiresome work. We talked at length about the methods of building the garden and she left determined to try her own hand at it. The results were incredible to say the least: during the first season of her *no-dig garden*, she produced nine kilograms (200 pounds) of zucchini and button squash!

This was just too much for the family to eat, so she made enquiries at the local health food shop with the result that she was able to supply them with vegetables to sell to others. She had actually made a commercially viable vegetable market garden in her own backyard, and one which left her with still enough free time to run the house and enjoy other activities as well. I wonder how many other market gardens there are like that, which can be established and yield so much in the first season!

It is now more than 11 years since I started the first garden: how wonderful they have been. A similar picture to one who is having music lessons — slowly at first, A, B, C, then with more practice and learning (and a few mistakes!) one becomes more expert. Finally after constant practice, you appear on the concert platform.

It is good to feel a little emotion at such an achievement — then to be asked to share your knowledge and experience with those who have not yet reached this goal.

It has been an enormous satisfaction for me. There are many people whose lives could be enriched by sharing something good. Sharing is caring. Many wonderful people have crossed my path to add another chapter to my life. To all those who have shared my garden with me I say thank you. For without them I would not have had this exciting, stimulating, interesting and happy life.

A GARDEN OF PAPER, STRAW AND HAY

HOW TO BUILD IT

Mine is simply a backyard vegetable garden, divided into several beds and maintained using organic principles. It is made without toil, without digging, without sweat and is easy enough for a child or old person to build. In fact it is so easy that a handicapped person or one in a wheelchair can build, maintain and enjoy a slightly modified version of this garden, but more about that later. For the moment, the design of the basic garden.

The idea is to build a garden on top of the existing ground. The *garden without digging* comprises rectangular beds raised above ground level, formed with old pieces of hardboard, small concrete clip bricks or anything to hold the rich organic moisture in place. The garden can be built for two types of environment: one to go on top of hard, rocky ground, or concrete, the other to put on a piece of lawn or existing garden. For a garden on top of lawn or existing garden, select a sunny spot, surround the area with a wall and spread a layer of newspaper a good half centimetre (quarter inch) deep. Make sure the newspaper is well overlapped to prevent the lawn from growing through. Do not use coloured paper or cardboard.

Cover the newspaper with pads of lucerne hay (as it comes from the bale). Over this layer sprinkle a light dusting of organic fertilizer or dry poultry manure. Cover this with a layer about 20 centimetres (eight inches) deep of loose straw and sprinkle again with some fertiliser. Finally on top put a patch of good compost, seven to 10 centimetres (three to four inches) deep and about 45 centimetres (18 inches) across, where seeds are to be planted. Two bales of lucerne hay and one bale of straw make a good-sized garden.

If you are making the garden on top of hard, rocky ground, or on top of concrete, the very first layer you should put down is one of old leaves, small sticks and pieces of seaweed, to a depth of seven to 10 centimetres (three to four inches). On top of this place a layer of newspaper, and continue to build as described above. See how easy it really is!

PLANTING

Now you are ready to plant the seeds. I like to make this garden at the end of August, when it is the season to plant summer vegetables such as zucchini, cucumber, squash and pumpkin. At the other end of the garden I plant about eight potatoes on the lucerne hay (i.e. under the straw) with a little compost around each one. This gives me an ideal situation for the rotation of crops: alternating a leafy crop with a root vegetable and vice versa. For instance, one follows potato with cabbage. Water the garden after planting the seeds and then according to need, keeping the straw just damp.

Many people have made this garden at different times of the year, planting seedlings, and had success. You should experiment and have fun in your garden.

After a few months, at the finish of the leafy summer crops, the layers of the garden will have composted down and melted into each other, and now the ground is ready for the second crop which will be productive during the winter months. *No digging is needed.* You just add a layer of compost or manure and plant your seeds of turnips, carrots, onions, spinach, cauliflower or cabbage.

Plant the vegetables in patches rather than rows and remember to rotate the crop!

CONSTRUCTING THE GARDEN

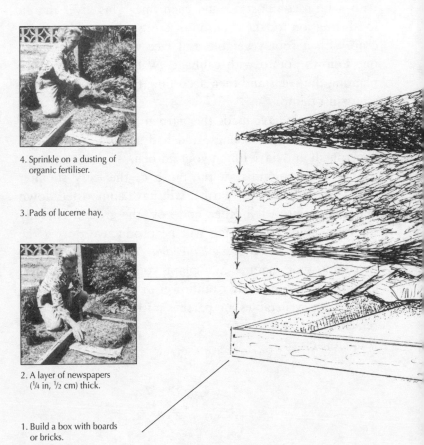

4. Sprinkle on a dusting of organic fertiliser.

3. Pads of lucerne hay.

2. A layer of newspapers (¼ in, ½ cm) thick.

1. Build a box with boards or bricks.

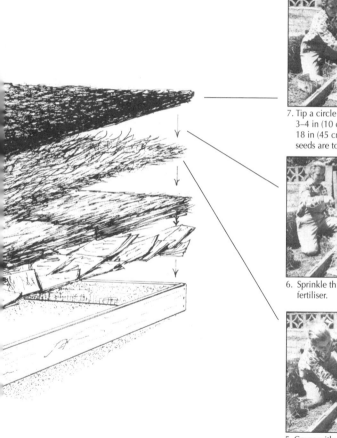

7. Tip a circle of rich compost 3–4 in (10 cm) deep and about 18 in (45 cm) across where seeds are to be planted.

6. Sprinkle this layer with some fertiliser.

5. Cover with about 8 in (20 cm) of loose straw.

Photo acknowledgement: Ed Ramsay

Potatoes can be grown in this garden throughout the year — make smaller sowings. As the potatoes swell make sure they are well covered with straw to prevent 'greening', which poisons the potato. Do not dig when taking them up but simply part the straw and collect your delicious potatoes — no washing is necessary if they are harvested when the soil is dry. During the winter months I covered the small area with a piece of hessian; the results were excellent.

Potatoes are a rewarding home garden crop when grown in small patches: they can supply potatoes all the year through. Growing them in the straw garden has proved a very interesting experiment and has produced a potato with first class keeping qualities. No heavy digging or washing is necessary before storing.

Cabbage should be planted following a root crop — sugar loaf or superette are my first favourite for a small garden and will grow all year. Chinese cabbage and red cabbage are a must for the delicious coleslaw needed in our diet. Grow several sage plants in your cabbage patch, as they help to repel white cabbage moths and other insects.

Tomatoes are a wonderful vegetable and should be planted following root crops, and with care they can be picked from Christmas until the end of June. The first seedlings planted at the end of August should give first picking by Christmas. The second planting of seedlings in February will give a good late crop. When the weather is cold during the night, cover the whole plant with a long dry cleaning plastic bag, which makes an ideal little glass house. Take the lower leaves off the tomato plant, leaving only the last 25 centimetres (10 inches) of leaves on the top. Grow a variety of herbs amongst them: chives, parsley, basil and French marigolds make a pretty, useful border around the bed.

Beans are a good vegetable and will grow happily in any well-drained good soil. Do not give them too much nitrogen as this makes the leaves 'heavy'. They need plenty of water during the hot weather, but you must take care not to water onto the leaves during the heat and intense sunshine in the middle of the day. Wait until the sun has gone down. If water is needed during the day, use a watering can and direct the stream around the plant on the ground — not on the leaves. In cold weather it is best to water them in the morning. This entire watering program applies to all vegetables and for the best results you should follow it.

Carrots and parsnips can be ready for picking every two months if the seeds are planted regularly in small patches. In very hot weather assist germination by covering the seeds with newspaper and keeping the earth moist underneath. At the first sign of germination remove the newspaper. Keep the ground moist and treat parsnips in the same way.

Sweet corn is a must in my garden. With a little planning you can expect three crops during the year instead of one. Plant only positive seeds, the first sowing being in September, the second in November, the third in January.

Celery is a worthwhile addition to the garden. You should try to eat some every day. The general opinion is that it is difficult to germinate, but this is not so when the soil is rich and healthy. I allow my best plants to go to seed, because good seed means a good plant.

Broad beans are another excellent and prolific vegetable. Plant first, second and third crops and make small sowings each time, which ensures picking over several weeks. When the plants are beginning to bloom, the young tips from the top of the plant may be picked and used as a vegetable. Also the pod, when finger length, is delicious when steamed whole.

Choko is a very handy vine — a good positive plant will remain productive for a long time. A negative vine will grow and look beautiful but the fruit is absent. So the mystery is solved when we know how to test our seeds and plants. The ideal way to grow choko is to have a free-standing frame well away from neighbours' trees and fences, etc.

Pumpkins need plenty of room and are an excellent vegetable to grow because of their good keeping properties. I have had them to seven and a half kilograms (17 pounds) in weight! They can attract lots of pests and the slugs and snails love to make the most of the shade and moisture beneath the leaves. We will talk later about pest control.

Cucumbers make a good addition to summer menus — when home-grown they are much nicer in flavour and quality. There are several varieties, all of them being good to eat. The cucumber likes fertile conditions — see the section on fertilisers.

Beetroot is so nutritious — both the bulb and the leaf. They like plenty of food when growing, particularly liquid seaweed and liquid poultry manure.

ELEVATED GARDEN

Could the *no-dig garden* be made or modified for disabled gardeners? Many suggestions were offered, some of them expensive, some of them requiring a great deal of labour and hard work. Then it was decided to try to build the garden on top of an old bedstead. It sounded ideal — little expense was involved, the height of the bedstead was correct for people in wheelchairs or for those who were unable to stoop down to ground level.

First, we placed it in a position where the wheelchair could move right around it without hindrance, and which received plenty of sun. The next step was to build sides onto it, which was easy using old hardboards and pieces of masonite — offcuts about 15 centimetres (6 inches) high which were wired and bound around the sides, foot and head. The garden could now be built in layers as described, following the recipe for hard, rocky ground.

Zucchini and cucumber seeds were planted in the middle, four potato seeds at the foot, and some carrots at the head. The cucumbers eventually draped over the side and some really first class zucchini made the experiment totally worthwhile. The follow-on crop was lettuce, endive, Chinese spinach, a few marigolds and heartsease for colour.

Another bed is currently being prepared to try strawberries; experimentation is such excellent therapy! One lady who came to visit my garden was most excited to see the bed being used. Immediately she saw the possibility for a 'three-decker' garden using an old double-decker bunk for two lucerne hay and straw gardens, and a smaller bed underneath for herbs. This of course is wonderful for garden lovers who have a very limited area, particularly in the inner city suburbs.

SOWING GUIDE

Once the garden is established, that is, after the first season, this should be your *vegetable sowing guide for temperate climates.*

JANUARY

All beans, cucumbers, Brussels sprouts, cauliflower, cabbage, radish, lettuce, tomato.

FEBRUARY

Sow seeds of: white turnips, all beans, beetroot, lettuce, carrots, celery, endive, leeks, marrow, onions, silver beet, radish, zucchini, sweet corn.

Plant seedlings of: broccoli, cabbage, lettuce, Chinese cabbage, cauliflower.

MARCH

Broad beans, peas, carrots, celery, Chinese cabbage, chives, cress, endive, herbs, kohlrabi, lettuce, mustard, onion, peas, radish, shallots, spinach, turnips.

APRIL

Broad beans, cabbage, Chinese cabbage, chives, cress, endive, herbs, kohlrabi, lettuce, mustard, onions, peas, radish, shallots, spinach, turnips.

MAY
Broad beans, cabbage, chives, cress, endive, herbs, kohlrabi, onions, peas, radish, shallots, spinach, turnip.

JUNE
Broad beans, cabbage, chives, cress, endive, herbs, kohlrabi, onions, peas, radish, rhubarb.

JULY
Beetroot, broad beans, carrots, lettuce, mustard, onion.

AUGUST
Beetroot, carrots, Chinese cabbage, chives, endive, herbs, kohlrabi, leeks, lettuce, onions, parsley, parsnips, peas, radish, rhubarb, shallots, silver beet, spinach.

SEPTEMBER
Climbing beans, dwarf beans, beetroot, cabbage, capsicum, carrots, Chinese cabbage, chives, cress, cucumber, eggplant, endive, herbs, kohlrabi, leek, lettuce, bush marrow, rockmelon, watermelon, mustard cress, parsley, parsnips, peas, bush pumpkin, running pumpkin, radish, rhubarb, shallots, silver beet, spinach, squash, sweet corn, tomatoes.

OCTOBER AND NOVEMBER
Climbing beans, dwarf beans, beetroot, cabbage, capsicum, carrots, celery, Chinese cabbage, chives, cress,

cucumber, eggplant, endive, herbs, leeks, lettuce, bush marrow, rockmelon, watermelon, mustard, parsley, parsnips, peas, bush pumpkin, running pumpkin, radish, rhubarb, shallots, silver beet, spinach, bush squash, sweet corn, tomatoes.

DECEMBER

Climbing beans, dwarf beans, beetroot, broccoli, Brussels sprouts, cabbage, capsicum, carrots, cauliflower, celery, cress, cucumber, eggplant, endive, herbs, leeks, lettuce, bush marrow, rockmelon, watermelon, mustard cress, parsley, parsnips, bush pumpkin, running pumpkin, radish, silver beet, bush squash, running squash, sweet corn, tomatoes.

Consult your local nurseryman as to what is suitable to grow in your particular area and climate. Again I cannot stress too much the importance of crop rotation. By alternating the type of plants grown, one keeps the soil in good condition and produces healthier plants.

MAINTAINING THE GARDEN

One of the most important things about the *no-dig garden* is just that — *don't dig it*! Digging this garden can spoil the wonderful work that Nature is doing for you. Our friends the earthworms do a wonderful job of cultivating the soil and do not like to be disturbed, so let them work in peace. It is easy to maintain the fertility of the garden by rotating the crop and adding when necessary compost, cow manure, liquid manure, lucerne hay, etc.

Watering the garden is an important duty. The general rule is that the plants should not be watered while the sun is shining at full strength. The best times are early in the morning in winter, and in the evening during summer. If you go away on holidays or for some other reason are unable to water the garden, then place plenty of mulch around the plants and water well before you go. Do not mind if a few weeds spring up as they can be helpful binding the soil together and so preventing a wash out in heavy rain.

Weeding the *no-dig garden* is easy. Because the garden is built up from nothing using lucerne hay, straw, paper and compost, there are no weeds initially and it is simply a matter of pulling up the baby weeds as they appear. 'Keeping pace' with the weeds in this fashion and pulling out a few each day keeps the situation under control. However, I do not recommend that you remove all of the weeds. Leave some growing, particularly around the edges as I have mentioned, to bind the soil so that it will not wash away during a downpour. A few weeds won't destroy the garden or rob the plants of too much nutrition.

SEED AND SOIL SELECTION
THE PENDULUM METHOD

*Behold, I have given you every herb bearing
seed which is upon the face of the earth, and
every tree, in which is the fruit of a tree
yielding seed; to you it shall be for meat ...*
GENESIS 1:29

Once we have established the soil for our garden the other
basis for its success is the seeds.

Seeds, both small and large, each hold in their case a
wonder of creation. From the acorn the oak tree; from tiny
celery seeds beautiful green stalks with their source of
health giving minerals.

Hold in your fingers the seed of an oleander. The brown
velvety seed is topped with an umbrella of silken threads
to enable it to float and land on some fertile spot to grow.
No man's hand is needed to plant it.

There is a special joy in planting seeds and eventually
watching the young green sprouts push out of the soil; the
beginning of a plant.

Some years ago I was given a carob bean which had
come from the Middle East. Knowing very little about
carob trees, I decided to plant the brown seed and wait.

What a rich reward has come! Watching it grow over the years has been an interesting lesson. It has grown into a very lovely tree about four metres (13 feet) high. As yet no fruit has appeared. The food value of the carob bean is very high. One full bean will sustain a sheep for a whole day. It has a delicious caramel flavour and its high food value makes it satisfying to chew.

In my own kitchen I have not used cocoa for years, substituting it with carob powder. The bean is large, brown in colour and quite sweet.

Although it is a little like cocoa to look at the food value is vastly different. The bean contains good natural carbohydrate, potassium, silicon, iron and a number of trace elements, as well as a considerable amount of the B-group vitamins, thiamine, riboflavin and niacin. It is rich in pectin, contains 7 per cent protein and very little fat.

In 1967 I had in my garden two very healthy paw paw plants about one metre (three feet) high. I always understood it was necessary to have a male and a female plant before one could expect a crop of fruit, but how could I find the answer? A chance visit of a friend enabled me to learn how to tell the difference.

Whilst walking around the garden I expressed a wish to learn how to sex paw paw. My friend said, 'I think I can help. Get me a small nail and a piece of cotton thread.'

A strange request, but I hastily produced both. A piece of cotton about 15 centimetres (six inches) in length was tied to the nail and the pendulum held over each paw paw plant. Over the female plant the nail rotated clockwise in a circle, over the male plant it oscillated from side to side, and over a neutral plant it remained stationary.

This was my first lesson with the pendulum. I reasoned that if it gave the answer about paw paw then it could be applied to anything else. So I started around the garden with pendulum in hand. What a revelation!

Why did some lettuce not make hearts? Why was that little cob of corn so thin? Why did the pods of beans vary? Why did a lovely Christmas bush in the garden yield only miserable, pale, undersized flowers? The Christmas bush was a seedling from my previous garden and I could not understand how such a poor flowering tree could come from a beautiful, rich, red, full-flowering parent plant. Now I had the answer: it was the male seed that had grown.

A busy time followed taking out the plants that had never given good results.

Later a science teacher visited the garden. She was thrilled when I showed her what I had learned and advised me to use the scientific names for male and female.

Male — negative

Female — positive

No response — neutral

Ten years of exciting research have followed, hundreds of tests having been made on trees, vegetables, flowers, seeds, soil, etc.

Dowsing, as it is called, is an ancient science and means to seek for something, especially with the aid of a mechanical device such as the pendulum. Water diviners are dowsers and so are those who locate minerals with the aid of a rod. Almost any object suspended on a thread of cotton, fishing line or whatever can be used as a pendulum.

I have used a small shell, key-ring, piece of amethyst, petrified wood and tiger-eye, all with excellent results. At the moment I am using a spring clothes peg in a length of cotton, which works well and has the added advantage that when not in use it can be clipped onto my sleeve or lapel, out of the way but easily accessible.

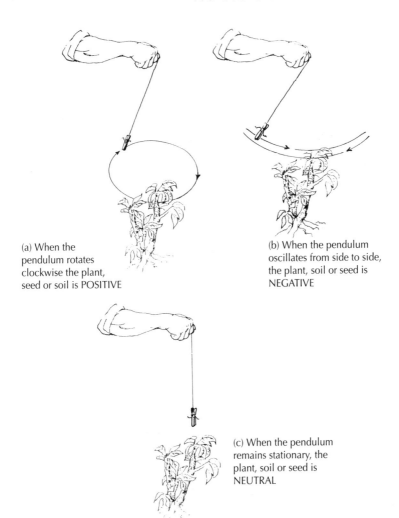

(a) When the pendulum rotates clockwise the plant, seed or soil is POSITIVE

(b) When the pendulum oscillates from side to side, the plant, soil or seed is NEGATIVE

(c) When the pendulum remains stationary, the plant, soil or seed is NEUTRAL

PLANTING

THE SOIL

Before planting anything test the soil. Hold a small clod of earth in one hand, suspending the pendulum over it. If it hangs motionless over the clod then the soil has no life force, no humus. Negative soil is indicated when the pendulum oscillates from side to side, telling us that the soil needs to be rested.

When the soil has become negative I build another garden on top. The area has not lost future production. In 12 months you should have another bed of fertile, rich soil. If the pendulum gyrates with a circular motion above the clod of earth being tested it is rich in humus and nutriments and ready for immediate use.

THE SEEDS

If the soil is ready to receive the seeds, you should determine before planting any of them which are the positive seeds and which the negative. As you would expect, the plants from the positive seeds will be more vigorous and better yielding than those grown from negative seeds. I plant all positive seeds with the occasional negative one put in alongside to test the theory.

To date the pendulum tests have matched the results.

Grow your own seeds

Allow your best plants to go to seed, but be careful to avoid hybrids. It is so important to use good fertile seeds for successful crops of vegetables. If seed is fertile and falls on fertile soil, it produces a good plant.

Remember: use the pendulum to test your seeds and plant only positive seeds for good results.

Ten different dahlias from one seed head

Take one seed head of a lovely dahlia, plant the seed and watch for the magic results. The first time I did this it was a thrill to see the variety of colours that came from a lovely pink cactus seed head.

The seeds were planted in my best compost garden. I think every one grew. There seemed too many to put in my garden so I shared some plants with friends, asking them to let me see the first flower.

Nine plants were transplanted into a good garden; one was left in the original spot and left to grow without help, except, of course, for water.

The plants grew quickly and made wonderful buds. The first flower was a joy to behold. Not one bit like the parent plant. It was the size of a large bread and butter plate of decorative formation. The colour one could scarcely describe. It was in tones from purple to magenta. The tips of the petals were palest mauve and a glow seemed to radiate from it.

One visitor to my garden described this dahlia as having a 'halo'. Another described it as iridescent. Imagine my joy — 10 different dahlias.

The plants I had shared had created much interest. The most outstanding was a glorious creamy white decorative with pale yellow centre, about 18 centimetres (seven inches) across, sitting on a strong perfectly straight stem.

Grow as many of your own vegetable and flower seeds as possible. Choose your very best plant and allow it to mature. Care for it — patience is needed because it takes just on twelve months from seed to seed. That is, from the time you plant your seeds until the time you harvest the seeds.

PEST CONTROL AND COMPANION PLANTING

PEST CONTROL

As a confirmed adherent of using only natural and organic matter in the garden, the question arises of how we can safely control insects and other pests without resorting to harmful poison sprays and killers. Bounteous Nature has provided us with many safe and effective ways to tackle these problems.

Many varieties of herbs are good repellents of insects and bug pests; by planting them among your vegetables you can control pests as well as having a ready supply of delicious herbs for the table. For example, garlic has a pungent aroma which is useful in deterring many flying insects. Rabbits do not like the aroma so keep this in mind if they are a problem for you. Garlic also has the effect of cleaning up the soil and disinfecting it. Tansy also deters flying insects so it is useful not only in the vegetable garden, but also placed in a pot on the window sill, or by an open door, where it will help to keep flies out of the house. As a bonus, the aroma wafting into the rooms makes them smell much sweeter than any commercially made air fresheners. Mint and sage when grown close to cabbage will help to protect them from the white cabbage fly. Thyme is said to help repel the cabbage root fly. Pennyroyal set on a path will exude a strong tangy aroma when walked upon and if near a door, or preferably on the step, will help to keep insects out of the house.

Marigolds are a first rate insect repellent as well as adding much colour to the vegetable garden and of course will help to bring the bees.

The roots of the French marigold secrete a substance which kills root-eating nematodes. The nematode, or eelworm, is a minutely small creature that can do tremendous damage to the plants in your garden. As well as this valuable function, marigolds among the tomatoes will repel the white fly. Basil is also good for keeping disease and pests from tomatoes. Rosemary repels carrot fly to some extent, however, if this pest is a particular problem onion can be employed as it has a stronger effect.

The slimy slug is attracted to rich soil and compost and what a pest he can be! Of the safe methods of controlling this unwanted and hungry visitor, you can use a strip of sand or sawdust around the vegetables. The slug does not like to walk over the gritty surface, and neither do snails. Another trap for slugs is a hollowed-out half orange peel under which they will gather during the night. Old cabbage or other vegetable leaves around the edge of the garden provide another favoured hiding place.

One method I have used extensively in the past to deal with slugs is simply 'hunting them down' with a torch at night, picking them off the plants. Once you gather the snails and slugs, pour boiling water over them — it is an instant death — and bury them in your garden.

Our common hump-back garden snail is actually an import from Asia and not a native species as some people think. Out of its natural environment and away from its natural predators, a population explosion has taken place, as any gardener will tell you. One day some years ago when I was busy in the garden catching snails, I found a new one with a flattish shell which I had not seen before. It was picked up and promptly disposed of along with the hump snails. What a mistake that turned out to be! A few days later I mentioned it to my neighbour who had heard that they were referred to as the native snail and that they were cannibals. As you can imagine, my interest was stirred. That evening while searching around the garden with a torch I found a native snail actually eating a hump snail! The two were put into a container and by morning all that remained of the hump snail was a clean shell. Excitedly I made enquiries at the Australian Museum. The snail I had found was Genus *Stragesta*, Species *capilacea*, or the native cannibal snail. Should you be fortunate enough to have such friends in your garden, treasure them.

Make sure there's plenty of ground cover and on no account use harmful snail bait. *Capilacea* like the damp soil under vegetation and nestle into small hollows, often taking their victim with them. They are shiny dark brown in colour and have a thin, flattish shell, the underside of which is lighter in colour. The body is dark grey and moves along to the side of the shell. If you do find any in your garden, then feed them on the hump snails and do everything to encourage them.

Another wonderful friend to have is the Leopard Slug. For a long time I killed these creatures. When the cannibal snail episode revealed so much, I felt prompted to question the habits of the leopard slug. Looking back, I realised that I had never once found one on a vegetable plant. They are scavengers, eating only dead food. Five were found eating a rotting orange. They clean up the garden of decaying vegetable matter and do a good job of eating leftover pet's food, bread, etc. Fully grown they can measure up to an incredible 22 centimetres (nine inches) in length. The Leopard Slug is a valuable helper to have in the garden and you should encourage them by putting out one of their favourite foods, stale wheatmeal biscuits. Always find out the facts about any new creature you find in the garden before destroying it. We can use Nature to fight Nature!

COMPANION PLANTING

Companion planting is simply placing plants together which like each other's company, in much the same way as we like to have neighbours with whom we are friends, and with whom we get on well. Plants are just the same! Here is a list of plants which do well together, and those which do not.

Asparagus likes parsley and tomatoes.

Broad beans like carrots and cauliflower, red beets, cucumber, cabbage, potatoes, leeks and celery. They don't like members of the onion family.

Dwarf and climbing peas like sweet corn and very much dislike onions, shallots and garlic.

Beets don't like climbing beans or dwarf beans.

Cabbage likes potatoes and herbs, especially sage, which also helps to repel pests.

Carrots like chives, onions, leeks, sage, peas and lettuce.

Celery likes dwarf beans, peas, potatoes and dill.

Cucumber likes chives, beans, peas, cabbage and potatoes.

Garlic hates beans and peas.

Kohlrabi likes onions and beets, but doesn't like climbing beans.

Leeks like celery.

Lettuce likes carrots and radishes.

Onions like the influence of carrots.

Parsley likes asparagus and tomatoes.

Peas like turnips, beans, sweet corn, radishes, carrots and cucumbers, but hate the onion family.

Potatoes like beans, peas, sweet corn and cabbage, but dislike tomatoes and sunflowers.

Pumpkin dislikes potatoes but does enjoy the company of sweet corn.

Radish likes most plants in the garden.

Tomatoes like parsley, asparagus and basil but dislike kohlrabi and potatoes.

Swedes and turnips like peas.

The chances of your success will be greatly improved if you keep this list in mind when planting.

THE EARTHWORM

I must mention another friend to all gardens and gardeners, whom we are apt sometimes to forget. He is the earthworm, who can help you to achieve amazing results. Earthworms will burrow tirelessly in the soil creating tiny tunnels which carry water down to the plants' roots and so decrease runoff in heavy rain. He eats fungi and harmful insect eggs as well as leaving a 'cast' from the soil that passes through his digestive system. This is a valuable additional fertiliser. Even when life is over, the decaying worms yield a source of fertiliser which is very rich in nitrogen. Worms are essential in the compost heap and if conditions are right they will breed there waiting to be 'transplanted' into your garden, where they contribute greatly to the health of soil and plants.

Naturally, healthy plants are more immune to disease and pest attack than sick ones and this is Nature's way of ensuring that only the best survive. Make sure that all your plants are healthy survivors by simply creating the right conditions for them naturally, and you can eat your way to health and happiness with home-grown foods.

COMFREY AND OTHER HERBS

He causeth the grass to grow for the cattle
and the herb for the service of man.
PSALM 104:14

COMFREY

Comfrey — the miracle herb — has been known, used in many ways, and sold for hundreds of years. Ancient physicians called it Knit Bone because of its remarkable healing properties. In more recent times, much research has been directed to finding out more about this miracle herb. The Henry Doubleday Research Foundation in the United Kingdom has been a leader in the discovery of the myriad qualities of the plant. No garden is complete without comfrey.

Comfrey belongs to the borage family and is a native of Europe. Because it is a vigorous grower that does well in most soil and climatic conditions, it is now widely propagated in many parts of the world. Its deep roots grow down into the subsoil bringing to the surface minerals and nutrients unavailable to plants with a shallower root system. The plant grows one and a half to about two metres (five to six and a half feet) in height and has thick, prolific, furry leaves. Both the roots of the plant and the leaves are beneficial to us as well as to other plants, as I have mentioned in the section on fertilizers. The plant, when well developed, will divide readily and produce seed heads, and the flowers are delicately pinky mauve or white. Odd seeds will sometimes self sow, but I feel that better results can be obtained by propagating the plant from pieces of the comfrey root.

The abundant leaf growth can be used in many ways. As a green manure, chop the leaves up and lightly turn them into the topsoil around plants. Quick decomposition will free nitrogen from the leaves and the topsoil will be enriched with calcium and other minerals.

The miracle healing properties of the herb are due to the active ingredient which is scientifically known as allantoin. It is used as an ingredient in skin ointments for the treatment of burns, wounds, etc.

The comfrey root is also used in ointments. Comfrey is the only plant that contains vitamin B12, and as well being a rich source of natural calcium and other minerals, plus chlorophyll. The early matured spring growth of the root can be dried and is available commercially from health food stores.

Comfrey leaves put through a juice extractor give a thick green juice which is very beneficial when used as a poultice to renew and repair bruises, sprains and damaged surface tissue. The leaves, after being crushed or heated with a little boiling water, can be applied straight to the skin on a bandage or cotton wool. Cover this poultice with a piece of plastic and then bind over the pad with another bandage. Care should be taken to avoid contact with clothing or bed linen as it will leave a brown stain which is difficult to remove. Such a poultice is reputed to be of benefit when treating tennis elbow, or other strains resulting from vigorous sport. The leaves were used on wounds during the Crimean War.

Compost making benefits from the use of old comfrey leaves, and a nourishing liquid fertiliser can also be made with the leaves. For complete information, see the section on fertilisers.

Pieces of root three to six centimetres (one to two and a half inches) in length, planted about six centimetres (two and a half inches) into the soil, will soon give new comfrey plants. Give the young plants plenty of sunshine and moisture, and a place to grow where they can multiply without encroaching on other plants. They will give you a harvest of goodness for the whole family. Comfrey dies down during winter, but will quickly make spring growth if kept mulched and given a dose of seaweed liquid or good compost. Unfortunately, the seeds seem to be unavailable, or at least I have never been able to locate a place that can supply them. Some nurseries stock the roots, or one of your friends might have enough to share.

OTHER HERBS

All herbs are a real delight to have in the garden. It is a good idea to grow them among your vegetables. They can increase the interest in your food and cooking with their delicious flavours, and the health of the garden with their beneficial effect on other plants and ability to repel insect pests.

Borage, the 'herb of gladness', is a particular favourite of mine. Tea made with borage leaves is very good for you, and the smallish leaves dipped in light batter and fried in vegetable oil are a delicious entrée to serve at your next dinner party. The bees in the garden are attracted to this delightful plant — how they love the little blue flowers — and its presence will therefore promote pollination in the garden.

Here is a list of some of the common herbs, their properties and uses.

Basil is a beautifully strong-smelling herb which loves to grow in strong sunshine. Grow it and eat it with tomatoes. When cooking with it, add the herb only at the last minute.

Borage flowers and leaves can be used to decorate salads. It is said to have a cheering effect on the mind and heart.

Chamomile is soothing for upset stomachs. The tea is made from the flower heads.

Chives have an antiseptic action like all the onion family and hence are said to help prevent disease. Marvellous in omelettes and potato salads, or anywhere a mild onion taste is required. **Onion** and **garlic** are part of the same family of herbs.

Coriander leaves and tiny fruit are used for flavouring.

Dandelion is wonderful added to salads. Dandelion coffee is an excellent beverage.

Eau-de-cologne mint should be kept in the bathroom or airless, stuffy rooms to sweeten the air. Chew to sweeten the breath. Brush your hand over the leaves to release the delightful fragrance.

Lemon balm makes a beautiful tea which is said to lift the spirits when one is feeling tired or depressed. Bees are attracted to it in the garden.

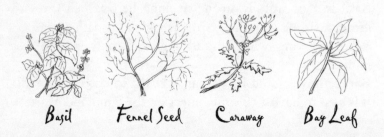

Basil   Fennel Seed   Caraway   Bay Leaf

Marjoram is a culinary herb as well as a tonic. It goes well with tomato dishes and fish.

Mint is one of the most famous herbs of all time. Everyone knows how good mint sauce is with spring lamb! It is said to be good for the mind and memory.

Parsley contains vitamins A and C, iron, calcium and phosphorus. It is good for the kidneys and nerves.

Pennyroyal is a dwarf mint with a strong flavour. Use a little in teas or drinks. It likes being walked on, and exudes a strong aroma when bruised. Grow pennyroyal in pots near your door, as it will help repel ants and fleas.

Peppermint is a popular herbal tea high in vitamin C and is good for colds and upset stomachs.

Sage leaves added to normal tea will strengthen resistance to disease. Gargle with the cold tea for relief from sore throats.

Tansy should be planted in a pot and kept near doorways and windows to help repel flies.

Thyme is good when added to seasonings, meatloaves and some fish dishes, imparting a pleasant taste.

Marjoram   Oregano   Parsley   Sage

Yarrow is a general strengthener and has been used by the Chinese for thousands of years. Yarrow was used by Napolean's army to heal war wounds. It helps to prevent colds.

Grow herbs in your garden because a garden without fragrance is a garden without soul.

FERTILISING, COMPOST AND HOMEMADE LIQUIDS

COMPOST

Compost is essential to making and retaining a good vegetable garden. *It is nature's supreme fertiliser*! Good compost is filled with every good organic material, minerals, millions of helpful micro-organisms as well as trace elements. Soils rich in organic matter are a breeding ground for some of the helpful bacteria and moulds which attack many of the fungi that produce plant disease. If you haven't been using lots of compost in your garden then both you and your plants have been missing out badly. This is particularly important when growing vegetables, since the more healthy the plant is, the more healthy you will be for having eaten it.

In a correctly made compost heap, Nature does all of the work for you, your only task being to provide the right conditions. Many things can go into the compost heap: any green plant matter (provided it is free from disease), lawn clippings, kitchen waste, fruit and vegetable peelings, weeds, seaweed, vines of peas and beans and so on. In a properly made heap the temperature will rise to about 82°C (180°F), and it is then that bacteria will break down and decay the vegetable matter. After some time the heap will cool and our friends the earthworms will move in, redistributing the material and 'cultivating' the heap. After about six months you will have a treasure trove of organic goodness.

The heap will rot down better and faster if you use some type of activator, such as animal or bird manure, or comfrey or yarrow leaves.

The top of the bin is covered by a hinged wooden lid.

Air holes are a necessity in the walls.

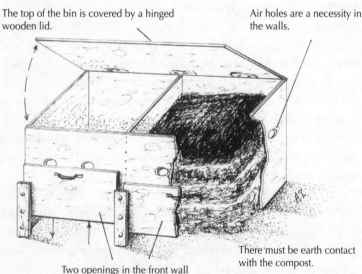

There must be earth contact with the compost.

Two openings in the front wall each 40 centimetres (15 inches) wide.

The advantage of a large bin is that it does give plenty of good compost after six or nine months, and allows you to be refilling one side while still using the already composted material which you have pushed over to the other.

Blood and bone is excellent for this purpose, while some people use fish meal, if they have a ready source of supply.

The most important factor in the construction of the compost bin is that the bottom of the bin must be open. There must be earth contact with the compost. I believe that magnetic rays, radiation and other forces come through the bottom of the bin to aid in the rotting process and help produce a really first-class result. Whether you purchase one of the commercially made bins, or build your own, it should be bottomless.

My own compost bin measures two by one and half by one metre (six by five by three feet). It has concrete walls approximately eight centimetres (three inches) thick and two openings in the front wall each 40 centimetres (15 inches) wide. A dividing wall in the centre of the box makes two bins — one for filling while the other is making compost. A piece of hardboard which slides down from the top of the bin on the inside prevents the compost from spilling out. The top of the bin is covered by two hinged lids. Air holes are a necessity in the walls and in my bin there are about eight holes, each the size of a half-brick. Without air, the compost will smell sour.

Use whatever materials are available to you when building a bin, but remember that air holes and earth contact are necessary. The advantage of a large bin is that it does give plenty of good compost after six or nine months, and allows you to be refilling one side while still using the already composted material.

When filling the bin, use only clean material — no food scraps. The first layer should be of coarse cuttings such as hydrangea, sweet corn stalks, choko vine or stalks, or old bean plant to a depth of about 25 centimetres (10 inches). If the material is a little dry add a little water. On top of this pile about 20 centimetres (eight inches) of weeds, some leaves, lawn clippings, vegetable peelings, or seaweed if possible. Next sprinkle a few handfuls of blood and bone, poultry manure, or whatever activator you choose. On top of this put another 25 centimetre (10 inch) layer of garden and kitchen refuse and so on until the heap has reached the required height. Don't forget to separate the layers of refuse with manure and a little lime powder or dolomite. Keep the layers level because the bacteria work horizontally and the earthworms vertically. Finally on the very top of the heap sprinkle a layer about five or six centimetres (two or two and a half inches) deep of good soil or sand to help retain the heat. Water the heap initially and thereafter keep it just moist. Lift the lid now and again, if your bin has one, to allow rain and sunshine onto the compost. The rain adds minerals and the sunshine will sweeten the mixture.

I have never found it necessary to turn the heap; I think that it rots better if you leave it alone. Once the heap has become very hot due to the action of the bacteria, and then cooled right back, the earthworms will invade it and do the turning for you. When the compost is ready to be used it is sweet smelling, crumbly black or dark brown soil, showing no traces of the original materials. If your compost looks and feels all right but has a sour smell, the problem has been a lack of air. In the next binful you make, it will be a good idea to make sure you have air holes.

Compost is critical to the success of the *no-dig garden*. It can also be spread around shrubs and other plants to give them nourishment. The earthworms which have bred happily in the heap while it was forming will now be transferred to the garden, where they will pull the compost down greatly enriching the soil.

LIQUID FERTILISER

The three liquid fertilisers I use are comfrey, seaweed and poultry manure.

Comfrey liquid fertiliser is made by taking an old metal drum or plastic garbage container of about 45 litre (10 gallon) capacity and packing it half full with *large* comfrey leaves. Then fill the container to the brim with water and leave it to soak for three weeks, until the leaves have rotted down. This stock liquid is mixed 50/50 with water and poured around the roots of the plants.

The poultry manure liquid fertiliser is made in the same way. Using a drum of the same capacity, half fill it with the manure and top up with water. Allow this one to stand for four weeks and use well diluted; the ideal strength in my experience is half a litre (one pint) of the stock solution to 10 litres (two gallons) of water. Again, pour it around the roots of the plants.

The seaweed liquid is made by half filling the drum with seaweed, topping it up with water and allowing it to stand for about three months. The beautiful rich liquid is very strong and must be very much diluted before use. Too strong a solution will cause 'burning' of the roots of the plant. The ideal dilution is half a cup of stock solution to a bucket of water, or 110 millilitres per 10 litres (four fluid ounces per two gallons).

The comfrey liquid can be used for pot plants if it is super-diluted. I have found that about 30 millilitres (one fluid ounce) of the stock solution added to five litres (one gallon) of water makes a nourishing mixture. Regular application of this liquid plus plenty of sunlight and love will make your indoor plants thrive.

LEAVES OF LIFE

This book is dedicated to the 'handicapable',
those wonderful people who have
overcome their disabilities.

FOREWORD

Every garden lover knows the therapeutic value of gardening. Fortunately the rest of the world is now discovering it and gardening is being used to calm and/or interest people who were disturbed or lacked an interest through illness, disability, or other problems.

A few years ago American research proved (if it needs proving!) that gardening is good for you. The National Heart Foundation supports this view with a rose called Young-at-Heart, which is their reminder to all that gardening is good for the heart. The 'Life Be In It' programme advocates gardening as a means of keeping healthy. Throughout the country horticultural therapy associations and schools are being formed to cater for the specialised needs of the elderly and physically or mentally disabled people.

Esther Deans' concept of the *no-dig garden* is tailor-made for these groups and, as well, has a wide appeal because it saves time and effort and is friendly to the environment since it keeps the soil in good repair.

It is logical to take the concept a step further by stressing the healing qualities of gardening. Esther Deans recognises that everyone, whatever their state of health, will find therapeutic benefit in gardening. This book sets out to prove that point and to introduce us to a happier lifestyle through the garden.

the late Valerie Swane, O.B.E.
20 January 1991

MAKING A NO-DIG GARDEN

I am writing this book especially for those people with disabilities which usually stop them having a garden of their own. It is for those who would like to watch a tiny seed grow into a beautiful plant, and for those who would like to be able to feel the earth with hands or feet. But sight is not necessary when one can smell the soft perfume of the tiny violet, the wondrous fragrance of a velvety soft rose, or feel the varied texture of the many plants and trees that grow from our soil. A simple garden can be made wonderful and can give so much happiness.

Our backyard was empty and colourless. After two generations of market gardens the top soil had been washed away because the gardens were not made on level areas. Because heavy clay made it impossible to dig I decided it would be a good idea to make a garden on top of the clay. I had a 20 centimetre (8 inch) concrete wall made around the proposed garden area and imported weed-free soil, which proved to be useless because without lots of fertiliser nothing grew successfully.

It was then that the inspiration came to cover that sick soil with lucerne hay and compost. What strange instructions, but I took notice and ordered a bale of

MAKING A NO-DIG GARDEN

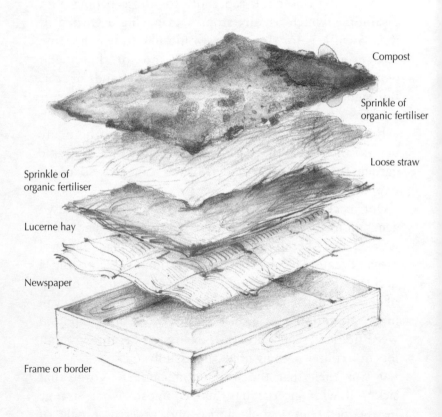

Compost

Sprinkle of organic fertiliser

Loose straw

Sprinkle of organic fertiliser

Lucerne hay

Newspaper

Frame or border

lucerne hay (when it was delivered the carrier asked: 'Where do you keep your horse?'). I covered the area with pads of lucerne hay, a sprinkling of blood and bone, a 20 centimetre (8 inch) layer of teased straw, plus a further sprinkle of blood and bone (you can also use chicken manure), and finally about 10 centimetres (four inches) of compost. The *no-dig garden* was now ready for planting zucchini, silver beet, carrot seeds and tomato seedlings. The plants grew with amazing results and were strong and healthy.

The next inspiration was to make a *no-dig garden* on top of an area of grass.

Make sure you have everything you need before you begin, as this makes it possible to have an 'instant garden'.

- Make a frame of whatever material is available — be it timber, old sleepers, or concrete bricks — around an area to give an easily workable, good sized garden.
- Cover the grass inside the frame with a layer of newspaper a half centimetre (a quarter inch) or more deep, overlapping well — do not use coloured paper or cardboard.
- Cover the newspaper with pads of lucerne hay as they come off the bale.
- Water the hay layer lightly (each layer should be lightly watered).

- Sprinkle the hay with blood and bone fertiliser or chicken manure.
- Cover the area with about 20 centimetres (eight inches) of teased loose straw.
- Sprinkle this layer with blood and bone fertiliser or chicken manure.
- Tip a circle of good compost about 10 centimetres (four inches) deep and about 45 centimetres (17½ inches) across where seeds or seedlings are to be planted. (If enough compost is available then cover the whole area.)
- Plant seeds or seedlings then water gently.

Hey presto, you have created your first *no-dig garden*!

Continue to keep your garden moist; in hot weather it helps to cover the seeds with paper or light hessian during the day, taking it off at night. Cover seedlings with an upside-down flower pot during the day.

A no-dig potato garden is exciting. Go to your greengrocer and select ten good round potatoes with 'eyes'. Place one potato in the centre of each pad of lucerne hay and cover with four handfuls of compost followed by a layer of about 20 centimetres (eight inches) of teased loose straw. Water gently and well.

After a few weeks the potatoes will push up through the straw. As they grow make sure that they are covered adequately with straw or grass cuttings, otherwise 'greening' might take place, making them inedible. When the tops have died down, remove the top layer of straw and your potatoes will be ready for harvesting. Store in a dry place (do not wash them) until you are ready to enjoy your lovely home-grown potatoes.

Because this garden is above ground level there is good drainage in wet weather. After harvesting, replace the top straw and cover it with compost. The soil is ready for you to plant beans, lettuce or any above-ground vegetable, such as sweet corn, broad beans or tomatoes.

COMPOST SOIL

If good compost is provided, plants grow quicker, are much more flavoursome, and are better for us. Working with good healthy soil makes gardening a pleasant hobby or interest. The worms that are so precious in the garden have plenty of work to do converting the humus to rich living soil. Take a handful of soil and see the tiny, white threadlike baby worms: put one under a magnifying glass or microscope and see the particles of brown already in its body.

All creatures we find in the garden make gardening interesting and it is fun to learn their habits.

WATERING

Watering a garden is a very special task. (Over the years I have made quite a study of watering my garden.) It varies according to the different seasons and the plants that grow during those seasons, so take notice of the plants' habits and the amount of water they require.

After a very hot summer's day I have the greatest pleasure in going to the garden when the soil is cool (at about 10 p.m.), turning the tap to about half pressure, and adjusting the hose nozzle to allow the water to fall down on the garden like rain. The resulting cool fresh aroma of the garden is a delight. If going to the garden at night, be sure to cover your legs and wear your garden shoes — sometimes the creepy crawlies wander about.

IDEAS FOR THE GARDEN

I received an enquiry from a woman in Brisbane asking if the *no-dig garden* could be made for people with disabilities. Until this enquiry I had not thought seriously about it. Jeanette, one of my helpers, mentioned the enquiry to her uncle, who suggested making a garden on an old bedstead. My neighbour had an old bedstead on which he dried his home-grown onions. Some 90 years earlier it had been a hospital bed, and after much persuasion I was allowed to use it. Little did I know it was to become so famous.

A row of old palings was placed on the wire of the bedstead to form a base and sides. It was covered with layers of newspaper, lucerne hay, blood and bone, straw, and was finally topped with fertiliser. The vegetable seeds that were planted on the bedstead grew into beautiful healthy plants. This method of gardening without digging or the need to bend over has wonderful possibilities for people with certain disabilities or for elderly people, as it allows them to share the healing benefits of contact with Nature.

OCCUPATIONAL THERAPY

A group of occupational therapists from the Julie Farr Geriatric Centre in Adelaide wanted to give many of their charges a new programme of thought and I was invited to demonstrate how a garden without digging was made.

The first *no-dig garden* at this centre was made for the television cameras on an old hospital traymobile placed on the lawn of the centre.

It was wonderful to see the happy faces of the 12 people involved when they were given newspaper, lucerne hay, straw, fertiliser and compost to handle. They were responsible for making the garden themselves, and planted small seedlings alongside new seeds.

Dr Farmer, the principal of the centre, observed the reaction and was most impressed by the active participation and obvious pleasure the residents found in handling the various elements involved in making the garden. He commented that he could 'see the wonderful therapy of this garden'.

Two years later, when I visited the Julie Farr Centre, I was overwhelmed to see the beautiful *no-dig garden*s that had been made by some of the residents in the sunshine of the open recreation area on the first level of the seven-storey building. The head gardener had made panels of concrete covered with pebblecrete about 90 centimetres (35 inches) high to be used for the walls.

This was a tremendous experience, all because a young therapist could visualise the pleasure derived from Mother Nature.

✿ ✿ ✿

Mrs Dawn Bennett from the Spastic Centre in Brisbane worked with many people with disabilities, and she thought it might be a good idea to have some *no-dig garden*s. While many people could only watch the flowers grow, others were able to be actively involved in the growth and selling of seedlings and some vegetables. Their first garden was made on an old table with sides built up about 20 centimetres (eight inches), with holes drilled in the tabletop to allow drainage. Other gardens were made in various containers, and they were all a success. One girl had a special garden of her own, at wheelchair height, in which she grew only strawberries, which she loved to eat.

A delegation from China visited the centre and were particularly interested in the therapeutic effects of such gardens.

* * *

Before you start your garden, sit quietly in a bright spot. With pen and paper plan your garden according to the space and position you have available, remembering that vegetables and flowers enjoy sunshine. Also, remember there are many ideas for the type of garden you can make in the section *More Ideas for the Garden* (p 127).

When planning your garden, take into account the location of the water supply, compost bin, tools and, most importantly, who will help you. To be able to share your garden with a kindly, kindred spirit adds much to the enjoyment of a garden. If you have no family to help, why not find someone nearby who would enjoy the pleasures with you?

Now I am going to take you for a walk in a garden. It's early in the morning. Just relax, close your eyes and let your mind wander about the garden.

The following poems were sent to me by someone who had pleasure visiting my garden.

THE CORN AND THE LILIES

Said the corn to the lilies
Press not my feet,
You are only idlers
Neither corn nor wheat
Can one earn a living just by being sweet?

Naught answered the lilies
Neither yes, nor nay
Only they grow sweeter
All the live-long day
Till at last the Master chanced to
*   pass that way.*

Whilst his tired disciples
Rested at his feet
And the proud corn rustled
Bidding them to eat
Children, said the Master, the life is
*   more than meat.*

Consider the lilies
How beautiful they grow
Never king had such glory
And yet no toil they know
Oh happy were the lilies because he
*   loved them so.*

Unknown

IS THERE ANYTHING AS LOVELY?

*Is there anything as lovely as a garden
   in the morning,
As a garden in the morning when the sun
   begins to rise?
When his face peeps out all rosy from
   beneath a misty blanket
And he stretches golden fingers out and
   pokes them in my eyes.*

*Is there anything as peaceful as a
   garden in the morning,
When the wind is still asleep and
   only breathes a gentle sigh?
And a mother bird is chirping to a timid
   little fledgling
As, with mother-love unlimited, she
   teaches him to fly.*

*Is there anything as peaceful as a
   garden in the morning,
When leaf patterns smudge a shadow
   on a sun-warmed crazy path,
And a little spartan sparrow, heedless
   of approaching footsteps,
Throws bright diamonds all around him
   as he takes his morning bath?*

*Is there anything as lovely as a garden
    in the morning,
When the flowers have a freshness and
    the grass is wet with dew,
And everything is quiet and the world
    seems to be waiting
For the sun to lift his eternal flame and
    climb his dome of blue?*

*No ... there's nothing quite so lovely as
    a garden in the morning,
When spider webs are draped like fairy
    curtains on the trees,
The quietness is like a prayer in scented
    incense rising,
And like a benediction is the humming of
    the bees.*

*Oh! I walk so very softly in my garden
    in the morning,
And I thank God for these moments ere
    the household is astir
And I bend to touch a flower or smell a
    lilac's perfume,
I feel in this dear solitude ... that God is
    walking there.*

Unknown

THE GIFT OF LOVE

John Ryan is multi-physically handicapped, and is blessed with a fine intelligence, a delightful sense of fun and the most wonderful gift of all, the gift of love. His compassion for suffering humanity and his understanding of human frailty transcends his own disabilities. John has produced a book of beautiful thoughts in verse, some of which follow. Proceeds from the sale of this book are donated to the United Nations Children's Fund.

THE OLD TREE

See that old tree?
It has many uses.
Children play in it;
They make friends in that tree.
When they fall in love
They go back to that tree.
When they have children
They will go back to that tree.

BY THE RIVER

I like to sit by the river,
Where there are old trees standing watch;
Where the green grass is a mat by the river;
And birds sing their songs of joy;
When I sit by the river
I think
How little we men are.

I WALK BY THE SEA

When I walk by the sea
I think of what I would do —
If only I could have this or that.
Then the sea comes over my feet,
How lovely it is.
It is the little things that mean
so much to us.

VEGETABLE GARDENS

In a *no-dig garden* there will always be something growing if the best plant, vegetable, or flower is allowed to go to seed.

> *Happiness grows from a very small seed*
> *So plant a few each day —*
> *They germinate with amazing speed*
> *And flower in a beautiful way.*

A salad or cooked vegetable is possible every day of the year — experiment, have fun, enjoy your garden. The following have been grown at some time in my *no-dig garden*: celery, lettuce, leeks, Chinese spinach, mustard lettuce, silver beet, chives, tomatoes, cucumbers, carrots, parsnips, zucchini, choko, beans, rhubarb, peas, potatoes, sweet potatoes, artichokes, broad beans, all types of herbs, strawberries, and other vegetables I fancied.

The *no-dig garden* is ideal for growing vegetables, but there are several other important points to consider before embarking on your vegetable patch.

LIGHT REQUIREMENTS

Vegetables respond well to light, and for this reason you must site your bed in an open sunny position. As you are aiming to provide your plants with as much direct sunlight as possible (especially in winter), it is recommended that you locate the bed as far away as possible from large trees with wide canopies and competing root systems.

Also, in summer plant corn in patches in which climbing beans can be grown using the corn as support, otherwise three stakes and wire mesh make easy support for beans and peas.

Grow a dahlia here and there — they give shelter to the small vegetables and add colour.

TEMPERATURE REQUIREMENTS

Cool Season	Intermediate Climate	Warm Season
Broad beans	Beetroot	Beans
Broccoli	Cabbage	Capsicum
Brussels sprouts	Carrots	Choko
Cauliflower	Celery	Eggplant
Onions	Leeks	Potatoes
Peas	Lettuce	Sweet corn
Silver beet	Parsnips	Sweet potatoes
Spinach	Radish	Tomatoes
Turnips	Vine crops	

Some vegetables require warmth to germinate and are very susceptible to cold weather, especially frosts. Others are cold season vegetables which grow best at low temperatures and mature during winter. It is important to know which vegetable belongs to which category and not to plant out of season.

SEEDS

Remember seeds are our future food — we must cherish any seeds from old varieties which have never failed us and have gone on and on for generations. If you have any old-time varieties to grow, allow your best plant to go to seed. When dry, take off the largest heads and place them on paper until thoroughly dry before storing in a jar.

The life force in seeds varies, eg corn and wheat keep for many years whereas parsnips must be fresh; carrots are fertile for about two months, beetroot for several months. Tomato seeds vary but use these from each season.

Select your best pods of beans and peas when on the vine and tie a coloured thread of wool around each selected pod and allow to dry on the plant.

Good soil with plenty of humus contains all the elements for healthy plants which in turn receive the benefit. Lightning, rain, snow and wind are all very important for healthy soil.

Hybrid seeds are lacking in the important life force which only comes into our plants from the true soil. Hybrid plants do not yield seeds that can be resown.

Use the following list of vegetables as a guide to beginning your vegetable garden. It includes those vegetables which are easy to grow in the home garden, and those which are popular in cooking.

BEANS

Beans are a highly productive crop for the home garden. They can be grown all year round in warm regions. Dwarf beans take eight to 10 weeks to mature and climbers about 10 to 12 weeks. There are many ways to cope with climbing beans — use what is available. Varieties to look out for are 'Royal Windsor' (dwarf string beans), 'Snapbean' (dwarf stringless), 'Epicure' (climber) and 'Scarlet Runner' (climbing runner beans) for cold climates.

BEETROOT

Beetroot is adaptable to all climatic regions but may run to seed if sown out of season. In cooler climates sow from September to February; in temperate areas from July to March; and in the tropics most months of the year are suitable for sowing, except for the wet season. Beetroot is at its best when grown quickly, and takes only eight to 10 weeks to mature. It responds well to doses of liquid fertiliser. Some popular varieties are 'Derwent Globe', 'Early Wonder' and 'Golden Apollo'.

BROAD BEANS

Broad beans are a cold season vegetable. They are suited to mild, temperate and cool climates and are sown from March to May and harvested in late winter and early spring. It is a tall, leafy crop and needs adequate growing space. Extra water is not needed until seedlings emerge in about two weeks. Some form of support should be provided. Broad beans are useful for soil improvement. Varieties to look for are 'Roma' and 'Coles Dwarf'.

CABBAGE

Cabbage is adaptable, and provides year-round cropping in all regions except tropical, where they are difficult to grow in the wet season. They require plenty of water combined with free drainage, and can be given regular side dressings of a water soluble fertiliser which has a high nitrogen content. Harvesting can begin from eight to 16 weeks after sowing. Some popular varieties are 'Green Coronet' and 'Sugarloaf'.

CARROTS

Carrot seeds will germinate in a wide range of temperatures. Plant from August to March and you can successively harvest them over most of the year. They should be planted in a space last used by an unrelated leaf crop. They appreciate regular deep watering.

CAULIFLOWER

Cauliflower is a valuable winter vegetable. It needs a cool to cold climate to perform successfully, but may also be grown in mild temperate climates in coastal regions. It needs the chilling factor for the flower heads to form. It is advisable to sow the seeds in punnets in autumn and then transplant into your bed when they are about 10 centimetres (four inches) high. As for all leafy vegetables cauliflowers require a high degree of nutrients to grow to potential. Harvest the flower heads when they are tight and solid for best quality. 'Phenomenal Early' and 'Deepheart' are well-known varieties. Plant according to family needs.

LETTUCE

Lettuce is a popular home-grown salad vegetable, and is suitable for either pot culture or to grow in your *no-dig garden*. They are quick growers and successive crops can be grown and harvested throughout the year. The crucial requirements for lettuce are that they are regularly and thoroughly watered and fertilised. 'Mignonette', 'Buttercrunch', 'Cos', 'Great Lakes' and 'Imperial Triumph' are popular varieties.

PEAS

Peas are suitable for all climates and are easy to cultivate. Timing your sowing is important as frost may damage flowers and young pods. It is best to sow in the warm northern areas from March to July, in temperate zones from February to August, and in cold districts from June to September. Erect supports for climbing peas, but dwarf peas are happy to climb around surrounding plants and vegetables. Dwarf varieties include 'Earlicrop' and 'Melbourne Market', and a worthwhile climber to try is 'Telephone'. 'Snow Pea' and 'Sugarsnap' (edible podded varieties) are both deservedly popular.

PUMPKIN

If you have ample space, pumpkins are a good vine crop to have rambling through the vegetable patch. They appreciate regular watering and fertilising during their growth period. 'Butternut' is a delicious variety to grow in the home garden.

RHUBARB

Rhubarb may be grown either from seeds or from divided plants from late winter to early spring. It is better to grow rhubarb undisturbed for about three years, rather than replace it annually. Although it prefers full sun, semi-shade is tolerated. It requires good drainage, regular watering and generous feeding and is adaptable to all climates. To harvest, pick stalks from the outside first.

SILVER BEET

Silver beet is not a true spinach, but it is often called so in New South Wales and Queensland. It is a rapid grower, being mature in 10 weeks. Because of its strong and prolific leaf growth it requires large doses of fertiliser, and is deservedly popular because of its 'cut-and-come-again' quality.

TOMATOES

Tomatoes would certainly be the most popular of home-grown vegetables (even if they are, strictly speaking, a fruit). It is a warm season plant, so take care if you live in an area subject to frost. To minimise disease problems, do not plant your tomatoes where they have been planted in the previous few years. Tomatoes are best harvested when really ripe as this provides the fullest flavour. There are endless varieties of tomatoes, which are too numerous to name. The best thing to do is to browse through the nursery displays, taking note of the type you want, the condition of your garden, the climate in your area and whether you wish to grow the plant in a bed or a pot. Some popular varieties are 'Grosse Lisse' and 'Apollo'. 'Roma' is good for bottling, and 'Tiny Tim' is excellent for pot culture.

ZUCCHINI

Zucchinis are a vine crop of the marrow family and are a warm season vegetable. They are a good plant for the home-style vegetable patch as they form low, bushy plants which take up very little space. The marrows are at their peak when they reach about 15 centimetres (six inches) in length, so delay harvesting until then. 'President' and 'Greyzini' are two hybrids worthy of note.

CHILDREN

It is, no doubt, a good idea for children to plant vegetables which they like to eat. Some that are easily grown and appeal to children's tastes are tomatoes, lettuce, carrots, pumpkin, capsicum, snow peas and potatoes. A fruit which is easy to grow and which will delight children is the strawberry. It can be grown in the ground or in a strawberry pot, and the children can observe the way it flowers and how the flower in turn develops into a ripe, red strawberry. They feel a real sense of achievement when — after watching their plants grow and develop, after watching little green berries form — they check the bush and there is a luscious strawberry ready to pick and eat.

FLOWERS

There is a need to add flowers to the vegetable garden. Having done so in my garden, one young couple found such peace there they decided to have their baby christened in the garden under the lovely carob tree — a little backyard garden can be a wonderful place. A little patch of sweet peas for springtime colour and fragrance, a few Iceland poppies for brilliance and the lovely open centres provide lots of pollen for the bees; pansies give edges a charming touch while heartsease are happy with everything that grows and give their own medicinal vibes. For summer be sure to have lovely dahlias, especially a single one here and there — they are a great favourite with the bees and also give moving shade for small plants. The old-fashioned marigold helps protect with its strong smell and adds a lovely touch of gold flowering for a long time. I do not advocate violets for a vegetable garden or any of the mint family, which spread quickly and spoil the garden. All mints are best grown in pots.

TOMATOES STUFFED WITH FRESH CORN

4 ripe tomatoes
2 cobs corn, cooked
1 tablespoon chopped onion
½ green capsicum, chopped
½ teaspoon vegetable salt
¼ cup French dressing
lettuce
mayonnaise

Peel the tomatoes and remove the core. Scoop out
the pulp and leave a wall a little less than
12 millimetres (a half inch) thick. Drain excess liquid
out of the tomato cups. Remove corn from the cobs,
add chopped tomato pulp, onion, capsicum and salt.
Combine this mixture with the French dressing and
use it to fill the tomato cups. Chill well and serve
on lettuce and mayonnaise.

SENSES IN THE GARDEN

Sound, texture and fragrance can be highlighted in a garden, as can colour, form and design. Each season brings forth wonderfully perfumed trees, shrubs and climbers. (It is hard to imagine spring without freesias, stocks, or boronia, summer without frangipani and mock orange, autumn without carnations, or winter without violets.) Add plants with aromatic leaves to the beautifully scented flowers, and your garden will be well on the way to being a perfumed paradise. Aromatic foliage is often ignored, and many spicy, woody and lemony scents are overlooked. More attention should be paid to these plants, and the following selection will guide you to selecting plants for year-round pleasure — to grace your *no-dig garden*, or to plant in pots.

TEXTURE IN THE GARDEN

Every good gardener knows the value of utilising foliage texture to create interest and variation in their planting schemes. Choosing plants with foliage which either contrasts with its neighbours or, at the other extreme, harmonises with surrounding plants is as important, if not more important, than choosing for flower colour. Harmonising plant texture by planting in groups rather than 'one of this, one of that' makes a dramatic impact.

To run your hands over a soft mound of creeping thyme,

or to gently feel the feathery foliage of German chamomile are delights not to be missed by anyone. Both hands and feet can be recipient to garden textures. It is lovely to walk across dew-laden grass early in the morning, or to run your hands along the shrubbery, feeling all sorts of contrasting leaves and plant shapes. By feeling your plants this way you will come to know your garden intimately.

NASTURTIUMS
Nasturtium leaves fascinate children as they are lovely to touch, and hold droplets of water after rain showers or hosing. Nectar can be sucked from their colourful orange, yellow or red flowers, and all parts of the plant are edible.

PLANTS WITH FRAGRANT FLOWERS

BROWN BORONIA
An evergreen Australian native shrub, brown boronia forms a sparse bush to one metre (three feet) in height. The scent the brown bell-shaped flowers produce in late winter and spring is extremely beautiful, and is carried on gentle breezes.

BURKWOOD VIBURNUM
An evergreen shrub which grows one to two metres (three to six and a half feet), Burkwood viburnum carries heads of white, delightfully fragrant flowers in spring. Cool climates are preferred.

CARNATION

The Latin name for carnation adequately describes the scent of this delightful perennial — *Dianthus caryophyllus* — as 'perfume resembling cloves'. The main flower display occurs in spring and autumn, but they do flower throughout the year. Carnations prefer an open, sunny position and do not like being covered by other plants.

CITRUS: LEMON, ORANGE, MANDARIN, LIME, KUMQUAT

Citrus trees are a valuable addition to your garden, providing an attractive small tree, wonderfully perfumed citrus blossom and edible fruits. They are not suitable for cool highland areas, where frosts may damage trees and fruit. Maximum sunlight is needed to ripen the fruit.

DAPHNE

A small, rounded evergreen shrub to one metre (three feet) in height, this charming plant has thick, glossy foliage and highly perfumed waxy flowers in pink or white. Daphne flowers in winter and early spring and is suitable for cool and temperate climates. If you provide it with a semi-shaded position with morning sun, good drainage and mulch over its roots to keep it cool and moist it should reward you abundantly with fragrant blossom, although it can be a temperamental plant and die suddenly.

FREESIA

Freesias herald the coming of spring. They are easy to grow and are showy, with their colourful and strongly perfumed tubular flower. In nature, only the white and yellow species occur, but there are many bright colours in the modern hybrid. They flower abundantly from late winter to spring. They pick well, and add a delightful fragrance to indoor flower arrangements or posies.

GARDENIA

Gardenias are handsome evergreen shrubs with sweetly scented blossoms. The perfume hangs heavily on sultry summer days. The creamy white flowers appear from November to March and the glossy deep green leaves are a perfect foil for them.

JONQUIL

Jonquils are an early spring-flowering bulb, with fragrant blooms like miniature daffodils. They look most effective massed or in clumps, and can be left undisturbed for years to grow in the one place.

LAVENDER

Lavender is a shrubby perennial growing from 30 to 90 centimetres (12 to 35 inches), and is evergreen with aromatic leaves. Lavender — of which there are a number of types — is native to the Mediterranean area and dislikes being waterlogged, so provide it with free drainage and adequate water in summer. It enjoys full sun, but is fairly hardy and will withstand light frosts. Pinch back the shoots to encourage bushy growth. All lavender flowers have a distinctive woody, aromatic scent when dried, and are used in pot-pourri and scented sachets.

LEMON-SCENTED JASMINE
Lemon-scented jasmine is a warmly fragrant, twining evergreen climber which flowers in summer and autumn.

MADAGASCAR JASMINE — *STEPHANOTIS*
Madagascar jasmine is a handsome creeper with glossy deep-green foliage which needs light support and training. Fragrant, white trumpet-like flowers are produced in late summer. It needs a warm, sheltered position in a temperate climate.

MEXICAN ORANGE BLOSSOM — *CHOISYA*
A small, bushy, evergreen shrub two by two metres (six and a half by six and a half feet), Mexican orange blossom forms a nicely rounded plant. Its leaves are pungent when bruised, and it develops a cluster of small, sweetly fragrant white flowers from early September

to November. It appreciates a warm position in the garden and can be grown in all temperate regions in Australia, and in sheltered sites in areas of high elevation. It is a useful hedging plant and can be clipped into a neat shape.

Mock Orange

Mock orange is a delightful group of shrubs. They are deservedly popular for their lovely late spring and early summer flowers. The flowers are white, and perfumed like citrus blossom. Pruning is done after flowering and old wood should be cut back at the base.

Orange Jessamine — *Murraya*

An evergreen small to medium shrub with a very strong scent, orange jessamine carries deep glossy green leaves and perfumed flowers reminiscent of citrus blossom. The flowering period during summer is long.

Pinks

The foliage on this short, tufted annual is an attractive grey-green colour. It grows to 35 centimetres (14 inches), and flowers are borne singly or in clusters in pinks, reds, lavenders and whites. The perfume is more delicate than that of its relative, the carnation, but even so it is well worth adding to the garden. Although pinks may flower throughout the year, their main flush is from July to October.

PORT WINE MAGNOLIA
An evergreen rounded shrub, port wine magnolia has small oval leaves, shiny green above and paler and dull beneath. The brownish flowers, hidden in the bush, appear from early September to late November. They are sweetly and strongly perfumed, and it is a useful plant for providing background structure in your shrubbery or garden bed.

POT JASMINE
Pot jasmine is an exquisitely fragrant evergreen climber, lovely wafting about and best suited to open spaces. It is quite vigorous and can be used to cover fences or pergolas. It is stunning at peak flowering, when the blooms almost completely cover the foliage.

PRIMROSE
The flowers of the primrose are a pale yellow colour with a scent similar to violets. It is lovely in wooded areas, under aged trees, or nestled into shaded positions on banks.

STAR JASMINE
A moderately vigorous climber with small glossy deep green leaves, star jasmine carries star-like, white perfumed flowers from late October to late December.

STOCKS
Stocks are a pretty annual, originating in southern Europe. Flowers have a sweet delicate fragrance and it is a vigorous plant, growing to 50 centimetres (20 inches) tall with a brilliant colour range. Stocks won the flower of the year award in 1976.

SWEET OSMANTHUS
The perfume of sweet osmanthus has been variously described as 'a blend of jasmine, gardenia and ripe apricots', and as 'ripe peach'. It is a sparse shrub with glossy toothed leaves, resembling holly, and clusters of minute white flowers. The perfume is very strong, and a couple of flower sprays are adequate to perfume the whole house.

SWEET PEA
Sweet pea is an outstandingly beautiful annual, loved for its delicate sweet perfume and for its wide range of soft and sometimes bright colours. The large pea flowers come in white, cream, pink, lavender, purple, red, maroon and scarlet, all of which are charming.

VIOLETS
There is nothing nicer in winter than picking a tightly packed posy of sweet-smelling violets to bring indoors and

scent a room. The fragrant flowers are mostly purple but sometimes white, and are borne above the foliage in late winter and spring. They are not too fussy about conditions, but regular watering and good drainage are advisable. They prefer a position in semi-shade.

WALLFLOWER

Wallflowers are annuals with a wonderful exotic fragrance reminiscent of spices of the Orient. The flowers come in a large range of beautiful colours, from yellow, orange and white, to red, brown and crimson. The long, narrow leaves arch gracefully and the plant is bushy: dwarf to tall types are available. They flower from late winter and early spring. Wallflowers are effective when massed in beds or in rockeries. They are a good cut flower for indoor decoration.

WAX FLOWER — *HOYA*

Wax flower is an evergreen twining climber with thick shiny mid-green leaves; a variegated form with a cream margin is also available. The clusters of pink, star-shaped flowers hang down, almost dripping with sweetly perfumed nectar in summer. The small flowers in compact clusters appear to be almost unreal and made of wax. New buds arise from the old flower spurs, so do not prune this climber or you will lose the flowers in the next season. It prefers a warm, sheltered position and takes well to pot culture.

PLANTS WITH AROMATIC FOLIAGE

BOTTLEBRUSH — *CALLISTEMON CITRINUS*

As its name suggests, this species of bottlebrush has foliage which, when crushed, has the scent of lemons. It forms a shrub to three metres (10 feet) on a short single trunk with many low branches forming a rounded shape. It bears a crimson bottlebrush from October through to November.

DIOSMA

Diosma is a low shrub to two metres (six and a half feet) in height and spreading as wide. It has fine, soft feathery foliage with tiny flowers in purple, pink and white shades in spring. The foliage is mildly aromatic.

EUCALYPTUS CITRIODORA

This species of eucalypt has a strong lemon scent when bruised or disturbed by light winds. It is a tall, graceful tree reaching 20 to 30 metres (65 to 98 feet) in ornamental plantings. Its smooth creamy-grey bark is an added attraction.

EUCALYPTUS NICHOLII

This is a tall, straight tree to 15 metres (49 feet) with a conical crown of slender branches with bluish-green narrow leaves. As its common name, willow-leafed peppermint, suggests, the foliage has a peppermint aroma when crushed.

Most other eucalypts have leaves which are aromatic when bruised due to the presence of oil glands in the foliage.

LEMON-SCENTED TEA-TREE

This is a small native tree to five metres (16½ feet) with a short single trunk with rough papery bark. The narrow light green leaves have a strong but pleasant lemon scent when crushed. The tree also produces masses of small white flowers in December and January. This is a small tree well worth having in a garden and, while it has a tendency to be sparse, regular pruning improves density.

PELARGONIUM

Pelargoniums are very useful plants and can be used as groundcover, edging plants, or in pots and hanging baskets. They provide not only a wonderful range of scents but also many useful flavours for cooking. Species vary in size and, although the flowers are small and undistinguished, they appear in copious numbers.

PURPLE MINT BUSH

This is another Australian native with a wonderful aroma from the leaf, this time the scent of mint. It is an evergreen shrub to three metres (10 feet) with delightful small, soft foliage and violet or purple flowers in spring. Other species are also available.

Take a walk in the bush and enjoy
the wonders of creation.

SOUND IN THE GARDEN

Plants can be grown to attract birds into the garden. Banksias, acacias and grevilleas are good varieties for attracting nectar-eating birds like honeyeaters. Many parrots are attracted by plants with seeds.

The garden can also be a place of different sounds, not only the sweet song of the birds, but plants can rustle in the wind, and wind chimes made of timer, metal, bamboo, or shells create varied sounds. The sight or sound of a waterfall in a garden brings forth an image of peacefulness and tranquillity. A bird bath is a must, as is a hanging food tray. Such additions to your garden are items of particular interest to children.

BIRDS AND INSECTS

It is not only the sound of birds which enhance the garden, but insects as well. Bees, frogs, cicadas and crickets all produce memorable sounds. A swarm of bees feeding on the nectar-producing shrubs create a wonderful low 'hum' in the garden and they produce honey and play an important role in pollination and cross-fertilisation of plants at the same time; and who could forget the deafening drone of cicadas on summer evenings?

Although all these animals contribute, it is the various trills, screeches, chirps or laughs of birds that are the most appreciated garden sounds. To attract birds to your garden, you should plant nectar-producing trees and shrubs such as grevilleas, banksias, eucalypts, correas, boronias, callistemons and some of the acacias. These provide the birds with a basic food source, but birds also need insects and other garden creatures such as grasshoppers, worms, cicadas and spiders.

No poisonous sprays should be used in any garden which will be visited by many birds. Some find food (insects) amongst the low-growing plants whilst others hang upside down to sip nectar from the brightly coloured flowers. Lizards sun themselves and sometimes beautifully patterned butterflies add their splendour to the garden.

Birds also need water and shelter in the garden for it to become a safe, comfortable environment for them. If you don't have a natural watercourse (creek or gully) through your garden, a bird bath or shallow water trough in a safe place away from predators such as cats is sufficient.

Finally, create dense thickets of shrubs and tangled creepers for safe nesting in a secluded part of the garden. Plant the larger grevilleas, melaleucas, prostantheras, bottlebrushes and banksias. This natural and bushy portion of your garden will become a refuge for birds. They can nest there, and materials for nest making such as bark, pieces of vine, grasses and dead leaves are readily available on site.

Noise-making Plants

Sound is a sensual pleasure we tend to overlook when selecting plants and trees. It is an added dimension to the garden which should not be neglected.

One tree readily available to Australian gardeners which creates a wonderful rustling or clattering sound in strong wind is the native eucalypt. Its leaves have a dry, leathery quality, so that when the wind rubs them together a papery-sounding rustling occurs.

One of the most beautiful sounding trees is the river she-oak (*Casuarina cunninghamiana*), and gentle breezes through the foliage create a whispering or gentle sighing.

Bamboo is another effective plant for making noise in the garden, producing a rustling in light wind. If planting this in the garden concerns you because it spreads so easily, try growing it in a pot. A large, wide, bowl-shaped container suits bamboo well.

The European aspen is a lovely rustling tree. Its small roundish leaves, broader than wide, with large rounded teeth are held by slender flattened stalks. It is this which permits the constant movement of the leaves and hence the sound.

If you live in a hot tropical or warm temperate climate, plant a grove of palms and you will be rewarded with their distinctive rustling sound when the fronds clatter on breezy days.

CREATING SOUND IN THE GARDEN

There are several ways to add sounds to your garden apart from using natural sounds. Water features are invaluable in garden making, because of the movement, light and reflective properties of water and also because of the gentle sound it makes when moving. In addition, it cools the garden in hot conditions. If you have a natural source of water in your garden you are very lucky indeed, but for those of us who don't, informal or formal pools can be created. Movement and sound can be added by including a fountain which sprays gently from within the pond, or by creating a cascade from one level to another in a series of ponds.

Safety should always be a primary consideration in designing water features in the garden, so:

• eliminate informal pools with no defined edge in the garden proper

- choose formal ponds or pools with raised sides or edges, and
- make the pond of minimum depth — 60 centimetres (24 inches) is sufficient for an ornamental pool.

If pump-driven waterfalls and fountains are desired, a pump would need to be installed and expert advice should be sought for its design and installation.

WIND CHIMES

Wind chimes and bells make delightful sounds in the garden. Many different types of materials are used for chimes, from tubular steel to pottery. Each makes a different sound, so it is necessary to listen to a variety before you choose one you like.

COLOUR IN THE GARDEN

BUSY LIZZIE

Busy Lizzie are easily grown plants which last for a long time and self seed, thereby producing more plants for the children. The flowers come in many bright colours.

COSMOS

The daisy-like flowers of cosmos will be an attractive feature in a child's garden. The plant grows quite tall, and is easily cultivated by just casting the seed onto the soil.

ENGLISH DAISY
The small 'pom-pom' flower heads of English daisy will delight children. Colours include white, pink and now red in the new 'Gemstone Collection'.

GRANNY'S BONNETS
The unusual flower of granny's bonnets resembles old-fashioned bonnets, and will provide interest for many as it is a prolific self-seeding annual which will provide plants for years.

PANSIES
Pansies are popular plants with children, probably because markings on the flowers remind them of little faces. They are easy to grow and have a gorgeous colour range.

PETUNIAS
Petunias are reliable and colourful plants which put on a good show without requiring too much care. Varieties are available in an extremely wide colour range including stripes, and some have frilly petals.

POLYANTHUS
Polyanthus are bright, cheery plants with a dense cluster of flowers. They come in a wide variety of colours, some in one colour and some with a star of contrasting colour

in the centre. If you are lucky enough to find *Polyanthus vulgaris*, the true primrose, it has a delightful perfume.

POPPIES
Who could resist these bright little beacons in the depth of winter? The solitary flowers are borne on long stalks and come in red, violet, yellow, tangerine, pink and white. They last well when cut.

SNAPDRAGONS
People love squeezing snapdragon flowers and watching them 'pop'. They are colourful, densely foliaged plants; tall, medium and dwarf varieties are available. They have a faint perfume.

STOCKS
The scent of stocks will appeal. Dwarf, medium and tall varieties are available and there is a wide colour range.

JOHN'S STORY

John was a student at the Deaf and Blind Children's Centre, North Rocks. They have very caring teachers to help the children staying at the centre and one of the teachers, whom I have named Samson, helped John with his garden on the old bedstead.

John loves gardens, and with Samson's help he was able to create a garden on a bedstead. The plants grown in the garden were very healthy with different shaped leaves, varied textures as well as distinct smells, helping John to learn more about the variety of plants that can be grown in a garden.

Other children at the centre have been helped with gardens by Samson, and they have been able to plant trees and shrubs in an area where nothing has grown before. The children enjoy touching the various leaves and learning the different fragrances which are an essential part of any garden.

HERBS

Culinary herbs are used widely in gardens as they are both attractive as plant specimens and useful in food preparation and flavouring. Herbs are usually positioned together in a bed as close as possible to the kitchen to enable quick access when cooking, although there is no reason why they should not take their place in the garden at large. They can be grown in pots, used as hedges or edging plants or, indeed, as part of the general shrubbery. They can also be used as groundcover or to replace lawn. Thyme, marjoram and chamomile make delightfully fragrant walkways. If substituting an existing lawn with a thyme cover choose one of the varieties of *Thymus serpyllum*, which forms a dense mat.

HOT, DRY, SUNNY SITE
Mediterranean herbs
(Grey, shrubby foliage)

Bay	Rosemary
Catmint	Rue
Cistus	Sage
Hyssop	Santolinas
Jerusalem sage	Thyme
Lavender	Wormwood
Marjoram	

COOL, DAMP SITE
(Green and herbaceous)

Angelica	Lemon balm
Balm	Lovage
Basil	Meadowsweet
Bergamot	Mint
Borage	Parsley
Chives	Sweet cicily (chervil)
Cress	Tansy
Fennel	Tarragon
Feverfew	Turmeric

Herbs have many uses and need not be confined to herb beds, however, if you are going to mix them in the garden it is wise to ensure the habitat is suited to each particular herb. There are basically two types of herbs — those which like a 'Mediterranean' climate (hot, dry and sunny), and those which prefer damper and shadier sites. The table will help you identify which herb belongs to which category.

The following herbs include those most commonly used and those most readily available at local nurseries. Specialist herb nurseries should be able to provide the enthusiast with a wide range of more unusual herbs.

BASIL

Common basil grows to about 50 centimetres (20 inches) high, with glossy green leaves and a spike of white flowers. Basil loves the warmer spots in the garden. Bush basil is a good specimen for a pot as it is compact. In cooking, basil goes extremely well with tomato, and can be used in tomato soups, sauces, salads and to make pesto.

BORAGE

Borage is an annual, varying in height from 30 to 90 centimetres (12 to 35 inches), with coarse, hairy leaves and stems. Borage is hardy and easily grown. It is a very beautiful plant. The little bright blue flowers attract bees in profusion. Sit nearby when they are in full bloom and enjoy listening to the hum of the bees. The flowers add a delightful touch to salads and can be sugar coated for cake decorations. Borage is known as the herb of gladness. It may self sow, so it will provide you with plants over a period of years. It can be used to flavour drinks and punches, and has a pleasant cucumber flavour.

CHAMOMILE

Chamomile grows to 30 centimetres (12 inches) high, with delightfully feathery leaves of the purest green and white daisy-like flowers. It can be grown in sun or semi-shade. A soothing herbal tea may be made from the flowers, and it is also reputed to ease anxiety and soothes and works as a sedative for children suffering from colic or earache. Some people may be allergic to chamomile. Finally, it can also be used as a hair rinse.

CHIVES
Chives are a type of onion. The leaves will grow 25 to 30 centimetres (10 to 12 inches) high, but may be kept trimmed to a lower height. The bright green, slender leaves are fine and hollow and taste of garlic. Full sun is preferred but chives do tolerate partial shade. Chives can be used in most savoury dishes.

DILL
Dill has finely cut, feathery blue-green leaves and small yellow flowers. Seeds can be sown in spring or early summer. The leaves have a pungent, bitter-sweet taste, and the seeds can also be used for flavouring. Dill prefers full sun, and the leaves and seeds are ripe for fresh use in summer.

GARLIC
Garlic has flat green leaves which grow to one metre (three feet) and die back after flowering, and has purple and white flowers. The bulblets should be planted in full sun, and provided with adequate water in a well-drained position. Garlic is used in many recipes, and is also credited with having health-giving properties.

LEMON BALM

Balm grows to one metre (three feet), and its attractive, toothed green leaves have a strong lemon scent. The plant has small white flowers. It is a good herb to grow in a pot, and has many culinary uses.

LEMON VERBENA

The lemon verbena shrub has lemon-scented leaves and needs to be grown in a warm sheltered position in full sun. The narrow lemony leaves can be used in pot-pourri and as a herbal tea. Pinch out new shoots to encourage bushy growth, and mulch around the base in winter to give the roots shelter from the cold.

LOVAGE

The dark, glossy green leaves of lovage — resembling celery leaves — make for an attractive plant. It is strongly aromatic and produces yellow flowers. It is used in savoury dishes, with salads and to make herbal teas.

MARJORAM

Marjoram grows 30 to 40 centimetres (12 to 16 inches) high, and has oval leaves with tiny white or purplish flowers. It thrives in full sun but must not be allowed to dry out, so attention should be paid to watering it.

MINT: PEPPERMINT, EAU DE COLOGNE, APPLE MINT, PENNYROYAL, SPEARMINT

Many types of mint are available. They spread by runners and are therefore suitable plants for pots. Each species varies in height from low groundcover to bushes which reach one metre (three feet) in height. Flower colours vary from white to pink, lilac and purple. Mint is a very useful herb for flavouring drinks, salads and peas, and for infusing in teas. They grow easily in a moist, sunny, warm position.

NASTURTIUM

The nasturtium has its origins in southern and central America. It is a strong climber with long twining stems, and is available with pink, white, yellow, orange, scarlet and red flowers. All parts of the plant are edible, and can be used creatively.

OREGANO

Oregano is a mat-forming perennial growing to 75 centimetres (30 inches), and the long oval leaves are dark green and can be either smooth or hairy. Its pungent flavour complements both vegetarian and meat dishes, and is traditionally associated with Italian, Spanish and South American cooking.

Parsley

Parsley is one of the most popular of herbs, and adapts well to container planting. It has a curly deep green leaf, and tolerates both full sun and half shade. When established, plants respond well to regular applications of a liquid plant food. When harvesting parsley pick the leaves from the outside of the plant, as new growth takes place from the centre of the crown.

Rosemary

The dense leafy branches of rosemary give it a somewhat spiky outline. The leaves have a pine-like fragrance, and rosemary is a very useful plant for Australia as it enjoys full sun. This is a versatile herb, and can flavour vinegars or soups, stuff meat, or enhance sauces.

Sage

Sage is a semi-woody shrub growing to 50 centimetres (20 inches), with rough-textured, long, grey-green leaves. It has vertical spikes of flowers in blue, white, or pink. Full sun is required, and these plants will tolerate quite dry conditions. It is traditionally used in stuffings and meat dishes but, as with all herbs, this is just a start for other inventive approaches.

THYME

Thyme is a small bushy plant related to the mint family and grown for its distinctive, warm aroma. Thyme is a plant of the sunny slopes of the Mediterranean, and is traditionally used in bouquet garni and in meat stuffings with sage and onion.

ZUCCHINI WITH HERBS

500 g zucchini
1 small onion, chopped
1 clove garlic
¼ cup butter
2 dessertspoons vegetable oil
1 teaspoon vegetable salt seasoning
1 teaspoon sweet basil
½ bay leaf
5 tomatoes, peeled and cut up
2 dessertspoons chopped parsley

Wash and cut zucchini into thin rounds. Do not peel. Sauté onion and garlic in the melted butter and oil until slightly brown. Add zucchini and all seasonings and herbs, together with a half cup of boiling water. Cook a few minutes. Add tomatoes. Cook a few minutes more. Add chopped parsley and serve.

SERVES 8

Teaching Children to Love the Garden

There is a wonderful variety of creatures, both good and bad, to be found in a garden. Children can learn that there is a common snail, as well as a cannibal snail that eats the common snail; that there is a magical process of the butterfly cycle, from an egg to a caterpillar to a butterfly. Give a child a magnifying glass to see just how beautiful the tiny flowers on weeds are. The wonders of creation are beyond one's comprehension.

The child should have the responsibility of selecting the plants, preparing the garden, planting, watering, fertilising and weeding. For children who are visually impaired, plants with fragrant flowers or aromatic foliage or those with interesting leaf textures are the best choice. For children with restricted mobility, annuals are easy to care for and can be readily grown in small beds or in pots, as will be discussed in the section on container planting. Other suggestions for plants and methods children will enjoy are scattered throughout the book.

❋ ❋ ❋

When in Brisbane recently I visited a school where blind children are integrated with sighted children. Try to imagine my experience when two pretty little blind six year olds were asked: 'Would you like to read to Esther a story about the dinosaur?' To see their dear little fingers reading braille was tremendous.

They had a dinosaur's cave made from hessian. A big cushion was on the floor and pictures of toys and dinosaurs abounded. I was invited to go into the cave, where growly noises were made to frighten me — such fun and happiness was a joy to experience.

The older class showed great interest in their lesson on the food chain. The special class was made up of two blind children, two partially blind and one sighted child, as well as the teacher.

Another delightful experience was to be invited to the home of a gentleman who lost his sight as a child of six. It was explained to me how difficult it is to learn to be blind after being sighted. Special schools and very special people are required to help the adjustment in such a situation. That gentleman has become a good pianist, and now teaches blind children to play.

When visiting New Zealand several years ago it was my pleasure to stay with a family who had a lovely daughter who became blind at six years of age following an illness. Her achievements are worth telling. After learning to be blind she became an excellent pupil right through her schooldays with the help of a very good friend: a guide dog was her constant companion. After leaving school she became a very efficient operator in the dark room of a local photographer. She was also secretary of the local garden club.

WHAT CAN LITTLE HANDS DO?

Children can have a lot of fun in a garden. They can plant seeds and watch plants grow from the seeds; they can see the busy bees at work, put down crumbs for the birds, wash the vegetables that have come straight from the earth, learn about the good and bad weeds or take a flower to a friend, young or old. They can learn about the various creatures we find in our garden — the beautiful butterflies, the wriggly worms. Hands and feet can touch the earth and feel the different flowers and plants: they can also learn how to water the garden to help the thirsty plants grow big and strong.

It is very important to commence teaching a child — whether they have a disability or not — to know the wonders and beauty of creation. To feel the soft petals of a flower without hurting the flower ... to touch the warm earth ... to feel gentle raindrops on skin ... to watch the trees in the wind: these are all wonderful learning experiences.

MIRACLE OF SPRING

There was a miracle of loaves and fishes
A miracle of water turned to wine
Through the bare earth a little leaf blade pushes
Slim as a sword and delicate and fine
From a brown seed no larger than a pinpoint
A leaf, a stem, a bud, a flower and then
From flower a seed in rhythmic rotation
To leaf and stem and bud and flower again.
There was a miracle of loaves and fishes
But I have seen the miracle of spring
The wonder that is life itself unfolding
I have no room for doubt of anything.

Unknown

More Ideas for the Garden

Remember that gardens are not made by sitting in the shade and saying, 'Oh, how beautiful' — plenty of love and care are needed.

COMPANION PLANTING

Experiment and have fun in your garden — a self-sown seed usually finds its own companion.

CELERY

When self-sown, celery decides its own companions such as leeks and potatoes. I have found it growing in the grass and even in the cracks of concrete.

LEEKS

Leeks are growing around most of my garden.

NASTURTIUMS

Nasturtiums are excellent, having a strong aromatic essence which passes through the roots into soil, thus benefiting other plants. They are also reputed to deter aphids and other pests. The white butterfly is attracted to nasturtiums for laying eggs, and the resulting caterpillar is easily seen and removed.

CABBAGES

The cabbage white butterfly is attracted to the smell of the cabbage, but if you plant marigolds with them they will disguise the smell of cabbage.

LUPINS

Lupins are a well-known green manure crop, which when dug in increase nitrogen in the soil. Added to this, they are a very pretty flowering plant. Save the seed of the best of your lupins for, although they are perennials, they fade out and it is necessary to treat them as an annual and replace them each year.

HEARTSEASE

I love to see heartsease in the garden, and everything is happy to have their company.

FORGET-ME-NOTS

Forget-me-nots are good companion plants as they give mulch and provide shelter for bacteria, which is useful to the soil. They are very easy to thin out and can be shared with friends. Put a couple of plants in pots.

SWEET CORN

Sweet corn makes a good companion for climbing beans, which enjoy climbing up the stalk.

Onions

Any of the onion family are distasteful to peas, and are not good companions to them.

Herbs

Herbs are beneficial in every garden whether they are grown with flowers or with vegetables. For example, marjoram and basil are good with tomatoes, and when crushed also repel flies; coriander, marigolds, calendula and garlic all repel aphids, as do onions and chives; lemon and lime balm attract bees; and both ants and aphids dislike mint. Pyrethrum is used as an insect repellant, and feverfew is not only pretty, but its aromatic foliage also makes it an insect repellant.

Some herbs, too, add vigour to surrounding plants — yarrow has this property. Borage has deep roots which bring leached calcium and potassium up to plant level, and as its leaves decay these minerals are made available for its companion plants. Valerian makes phosphorus more available to its companions and also attracts earthworms.

WHEELCHAIR ACCESS

If the gardener moves around in a wheelchair, paths need to be smooth and wide enough for the wheelchair, with ramps to move to different levels. Raised garden beds make it easier for people who cannot bend over. As well as the bedstead approach mentioned earlier, there are other ways of building a garden.

Garden beds can be made as part of a retaining wall, breaking the starkness of the wall with splashes of colour, creating interest and endless pleasure. The garden is at a comfortable level to stand and work and is not very wide, making it easier to reach the back of the garden bed.

A garden shed with benches at wheelchair height is great: it can become your own den. A chair or wheelchair placed under the bench means that the work area is easily reached. Pots or timber boxes can be used for growing a variety of shade plants, including ferns. Tools can be stored on the shelves where they are always ready to use.

PLANTS IN POTS

Many different species of plant can now be grown effectively in pots. For those people who are not mobile enough to produce a *no-dig garden*, growing annuals, vegetables and shrubs in pots is a solution. For people with disabilities consideration must be given to the weight and movability of the pot, and to methods of watering.

You should aim to have the containers as light and as easy to move as possible. For those who like the terracotta look, terracotta-coloured plastic pots are ideal. These look like terracotta and are made in many different shapes from wide shallow bowls to the traditional deep pot.

There is also a fibreglass pot available which has the appearance of concrete but is very lightweight. Hanging baskets lined with bark or fibre provide a relatively light container in which to grow trailing plants. Although these suggestions are helpful in keeping weight down, once the potting mix has been added to your container it becomes heavier and awkward to handle. The job of moving and watering plants needs to be made easier for people with mobility problems.

To make a pot easier to move you could attach casters to the bottom of a wooden planter box and place your pot inside the planter. This makes your plant more mobile and more attractive. Otherwise, you could arrange several plants on a low trolley with wheels or casters.

The following list may help you to choose suitable specimens for gardening in pots.

AZALEAS

Azaleas make perfect pot specimens because of their shallow root system. Azaleas provide a good splash of colour in the spring — even a tiny plant in a pot rewards you with masses of blooms — so really they are superb container plants.

BULBS

Try bulbs massed on their own or group them with other plants. Crocus, hyacinth, ipheion, bluebells, grape hyacinth and snowdrops are all suitable for small pots. For larger containers ranunculus, tulips, daffodils, jonquils, hippeastrum, agapanthus and clivea are effective. Tulips are lovely crammed together in a wide, shallow pot with alyssum frothing over the sides. You could perhaps combine daffodils or jonquils with floss flower.

Bulbs, too, are fascinating plants for children to learn about, the bulb itself being the entire food storage unit for the plant. Freesias are foolproof and provide a delightful spring perfume. Others which would appeal to children are jonquils, ipheion, bluebells and grape hyacinths.

To make a pot easier to move, you could attach casters at the bottom.

CITRUS

Citrus trees in pots are wonderful for many reasons. They have attractive evergreen foliage and heavenly scented blossoms, and fruit which is both decorative and edible. The smaller growing kumquats are the most obvious choice for a tub, while mandarins are a good choice for a large tub in a sunny position.

NATIVES

Lillypillies are shrubby plants that take well to container growing and appreciate being pruned. Once pruned, their fresh, reddish new growth is a delight, and they also produce a lovely oval berry in late summer and autumn.

The native rhododendron pots up effectively and the cluster of rich bell-shaped flowers is spectacular in autumn.

The brown boronia is easier to grow in a pot than in the ground as you can control the water supply and its perfume is, in my opinion, the loveliest of all the scented shrubs.

The little purple native daisy is a pretty spillover plant for a shallow pot.

VEGETABLES

Most vegetables can be grown in pots providing you place them in a sunny position. An ideal tomato for containers is 'Dwarf Cherry' which has an abundance of small, decorative fruit, a bushy habit and does not require staking.

Carrots can be grown in a deep pot and lettuce massed in a low, shallow trough are most attractive and can be harvested in a matter of weeks after planting seedlings. Nurseries now sell several different varieties of lettuce in one punnet which enables you to pick lettuce over a long period of time because each type develops at a different rate and provides you with a variety in taste as well. Snow peas can be planted in a long oblong trough and placed against a sunny balcony; the tendrils of the plant will climb up the railings, which act as a trellis. All varieties of herbs are also wonderful for pots, and they can be conveniently placed as close to the kitchen door as possible.

SEEDS AND SPROUTS

Growing seeds and beans indoors is an alternative for anyone with very restricted mobility who cannot maintain a garden plot or pots. Mustard or cress seeds, available in sachets from nurseries, can be grown indoors in a sunny position on wet cotton wool. Avocado seeds placed on the top of a jar of water will sprout readily — first the roots will appear, followed by the stem and leaves. The plant can be potted up when strong enough and in time planted out in the garden, where it will grow and eventually bear fruit (if you live in the warm temperate to tropical areas of Australia).

Beans, either soya or mung, alfalfa or lentil, will sprout easily. Buy seeds from a health food store which are packaged with the guarantee that they are unpolluted and free from pesticides. Soak the seeds for about 12 hours, then drain off the dirty water. Place the seeds in a large, clean jar and cover the jar with fine net or a piece of stocking. Change the water twice each day. In three days the seeds will sprout. The food value of sprouts is unsurpassed. Whenever the sprouts and roots have reached the desired length they can be eaten.

WINDOW BOXES

Window boxes are a good way of enjoying plants and having them within easy reach. Flowers or plants with interesting leaves can be grown to brighten a room, and herbs can be grown to add flavour and interest to the kitchen (see the *Herbs* section for more ideas).

Many other plants can be planted in pots: perfumed shrubs such as gardenias; plants with wonderful flowers such as hydrangeas, daisies, pelargonium, or fuchsias, and don't forget those with foliage which makes a noise in light breeze such as bamboo. The list for container planting is endless. It is simply a matter of personal preference, a little imagination and placing the plant in conditions which are suited to it.

HANGING BASKETS

Hanging baskets will accommodate any plant that will grow in a pot, but for decorative purposes trailing plants are best. Ivy-leafed geraniums are perfect specimens for baskets in a sunny position, and provide a brilliant display. They come in whites, pinks, purples and reds and their glossy, bright green foliage is a lovely foil for their brightly coloured flowers.

If you live in a tropical climate or have a warm sheltered position in a temperate coastal area, use bougainvillea 'Rosenka' in a hanging basket. It is one of the smaller growers, ideally suited to container growing, and has lovely apricot-coloured flowers.

Ferns also adapt well to hanging baskets, and are suited to fully shaded positions or dappled light. Keep them moist at all times.

Hanging baskets and pot specimens dry out much quicker than those in the garden, so it is crucial to check whether the plant needs moisture. One way to determine whether the plant needs water is to place your index finger into the potting mix: if it is dry to the knuckle it needs water.

A long-handled hose or 'watering wand' will make watering hanging baskets much easier if you are in a wheelchair. Alternatively, if your pots and hanging baskets are under a pergola, the system of black hosing now available at nurseries can be attached to the pergola and the nozzles fitted directly above your baskets. This makes watering them as simple as turning on your tap.

Hanging baskets can be made more accessible by attaching them to a pulley system. You can lower them to check on moisture levels in the potting mix, water them if necessary, then raise them again by pulling the rope.

FUNCTIONAL USE OF FOLIAGE

Plant texture can be used not only for the pleasure of touch, it can also define boundaries, mark positions and create limits to pathways and walkways: particularly useful for people with some type of visual impairment.

Paths and walkways can be created by forming side plantings of low-growing shrubs with distinctive foliage. One example of a suitable plant would be *Grevillea juniperina*. Ensure that the specimens you choose are not too prickly. Choose a plant distinctive enough to indicate the presence of a boundary without resorting to something dangerous.

To mark a position in a garden, select a shrub which grows to about one and a half to two metres (five to six and a half feet) tall, with distinctive foliage. Once again, the grevilleas spring to mind. Boundaries can be defined by planting textured hedges. If your garden has been divided into sections — perhaps lawn, vegetable patch and flower garden — hedges can be planted to define and divide these sections. Use a dense, small-leafed, tightly foliaged plant such as English box or box-leafed honeysuckle. Once established, these boundaries will act as tactile guides leading from one area of the garden to another. Hedges require a lot of maintaining, but once they have been established aim to keep them clipped to about hip level to act as a guide.

CARRY BAG

A material carry bag for tools and weeds is most useful. It is strong, and the material has a plastic lining to help protect it so that the bag will last longer. It can be laid out flat to be used, and the large handles allow it to be picked up easily, scooping up the weeds and taking them away.

THE STORY OF PETER MEAGHER
AND HIS *NO-DIG GARDEN*

You cannot give happiness to others without getting some yourself.

Peter is physically spastic, well educated, and always interested in learning and seeking new experiences. Peter married a very loving and caring woman, Janet, and they made their home at Engadine, a suburb of Sydney. Later Janet and Peter were blessed with a bright and healthy son, Timothy.

Unfortunately, the land surrounding their home was impossible to dig and their dream of having a garden seemed to finish. However, on telling their disappointment to friends, one said: 'Why not try Esther Deans' idea of making gardens without digging?'

I learned about Peter Meagher and his wonderful garden through an article written about him in a local newspaper. The story told of Peter's garden, which had been made on very poor soil that was impossible to dig because of heavy clay and bad drainage. From this terrible start Peter has produced a beautiful garden with award-winning flowers and vegetables.

The awards, which included 85 first, second and champion places, tell an incredible story. Not only did he transform an empty backyard, he grew various plants in pots and sold many at local shows and fetes under the banner 'Peter's Plants', which became well known because they always grew. Peter made sure the plants were growing in good soil.

Peter also had some other outside interests, besides being employed by the Sydney City Council. He accepted the position of Treasurer of the Geranium Society, and is a member of the Engadine Lawn Bowling Club. Peter is a very happy family man, interested in life to a great degree.

It was rewarding to visit Peter's garden, and to meet his wife Janet and son Timothy, and to see for myself what has happened to an empty backyard. Eventually, Don Burke on his TV show 'Burke's Backyard' showed to all people just how people with a disability can make a garden.

FROM GARDEN TO KITCHEN

HONEY-GLAZED CARROTS WITH MINT

6 medium-sized carrots, halved
2 dessertspoons butter
½ teaspoon dry mint leaves
2 dessertspoons honey
½ teaspoon vegetable salt

Wash carrots thoroughly and halve. Cook in the smallest possible amount of water until tender and allow to drain. Melt butter in pan. Stir in mint leaves and let stand for a few minutes. Blend in honey and vegetable salt. Bring to boil. Add carrots and simmer a few minutes until glazed.

SERVES 4

LEMON-HERB BUTTER

½ cup soft butter or margarine
1 tablespoon grated lemon rind
½ teaspoon dried basil
1 teaspoon snipped parsley
½ teaspoon snipped chives

Work the butter in a small dish until creamy.
Add lemon rind and herbs and refrigerate for
several hours before use. Use it to spread on hot
cooked vegetables.

CASSEROLE COOKING

You can casserole waterlessly by grating root
vegetables and slicing or chopping the more
succulent types. If you place a lettuce leaf on the
bottom of the casserole you will need very little
water. Fill the casserole to the top, cover tightly and
then bake in a moderate oven.

PUMPKIN PIE

2 eggs
½ cup brown sugar
½ cup milk
1 cup mashed cooked pumpkin
1 teaspoon mixed spice
pinch salt
some blanched almonds

Use normal ingredients for standard pie crust pastry.
Line a 23 centimetre (9 inch) pie plate with pastry.
Beat the eggs, adding sugar and milk, then the

mashed pumpkin, spice and salt. Mix thoroughly and put into pastry case. Arrange the almonds on top in a decorative pattern and bake in a moderate oven for about 45 minutes. Allow to cool and serve topped with a little cream. The basic method for cooking pumpkin is to remove the skin and seeds and cut into conveniently sized pieces.

SAUTÉED EGGPLANT

1 medium-sized onion, diced
vegetable oil
vegetable salt
1 tablespoon milk
2 medium-sized tomatoes, skinned and finely chopped
2 medium-sized eggplants

Fry the diced onion in a little oil. Add vegetable salt to taste, milk and tomatoes. Cook for about ten minutes. Slice eggplants into thickish rounds and cook in oil until they are golden brown in colour. Pour the sauce over them. Cover with a lid and cook until soft.

SERVES 4

❀ ❀ ❀

Herb teas are so refreshing when the herbs are picked from your garden.

❋ ❋ ❋

This book cannot be finished without telling this beautiful story.

A dear lady who spent 20 years of her life in an iron lung as a result of polio had decided that she would like to do something to show the gratitude she felt for all the help received over the years. She asked all her visitors and helpers to save their used stamps so that the money from the sale of the stamps could be given to charity.

The request passed from person to person, with Sunday school children being asked to collect used stamps from their parents. Office workers and people working in clubs and shops also joined in the collection. The result was overwhelming.

Stamps arrived by the bagful. Another patient at the hospital, who spent her days in a wheelchair, was able to trim the stamps and prepare them for sale. Stamp saving has now become an integral part of therapy there.

❋ ❋ ❋

Because of all the wonderful stories you have read, I am sure you will agree words like 'handicapped' and 'disabled' do not apply. Perhaps we should say 'handicapable'.

I dedicate this book to all handicapable people, with many blessings.

ACKNOWLEDGMENTS

NO-DIG GARDENING

Thanks to the numerous people who have contributed by sharing the garden and for the success that many have enjoyed with the *no-dig garden*.

My special thanks to Vivian Malfroy, Ruth Swan, Jeanette Percy, John Miller and Christopher Atkins.

LEAVES OF LIFE

Thanks to the numerous people who have contributed to the writing of this special book — to the therapists who have used the no-dig method of gardening to assist people with problems to experience the healing touch of mother earth.

My special thanks to my husband Tom for his constant help, endless typing and understanding.

My appreciation and grateful thanks go to John Miller, who inspired me to write my first two books — *Esther Deans' Gardening Book: Growing Without Digging* and *Esther Deans' Garden Cook Book: From Garden to Kitchen* — and for his confidence and encouragement to me to write this third book.

For those interested in contacting other garden enthusiasts, why not contact:

Australian Horticultural Correspondence School
264 Swansea Road
Lilydale Victoria 3140
Phone: (03) 9736 1882

What a wonderful inspiration John Mason of Victoria had to start a correspondence school for gardeners. It has meant so much to many people, especially those with a disability, to be able to have contact with others.

INDEX

This book is not intended to be comprehensive, but rather indicates popular plants, and those which it may be difficult to track down. Scientific names are provided for the more unusual plants.

Page numbers of diagrams are in *italics*.